THE
QUEEN'S HOUSE
GREENWICH

Pieter van der Merwe

SCALA

QUEEN'S
HOUSE
GREENWICH

This edition © Scala Arts & Heritage Publishers Ltd 2017
Text © National Maritime Museum 2012
Illustrations © National Maritime Museum

First published in 2012
Updated in 2017

Scala Arts & Heritage Publishers Ltd
10 Lion Yard, Tremadoc Road
London sw4 7nq
www.scalapublishers.com

In association with Royal Museums Greenwich, the group
name for the National Maritime Museum, Royal Observatory,
Queen's House and *Cutty Sark*.

ISBN 978 1 85759 753 0

Project editor: Sandra Pisano
Copy editor: Sarah Kane
Designer: Andrew Shoolbred
Printed and bound in Italy

10 9 8 7 6 5 4 3 2

Every effort has been made to acknowledge correct copyright
of images where applicable. Any errors or omissions are
unintentional and should be notified to the Publisher, who
will arrange for corrections to appear in any reprints.

Front cover: The 'Tulip Stairs', f7001
Inside covers: 'A View of Greenwich, Deptford and London, taken from
Flamsteads Hill in Greenwich Park', by E. Kinhall, *c.*1750, pad2182
Page 1: Inigo Jones (1573–1652), attributed to John Michael Rysbrack, scu0033
Pages 2–3: The Queen's House from the Park, l4251-009 (see p. 9)
Page 20: Elizabeth I, the 'Armada Portrait'. Acquired with the support of the
Heritage Lottery Fund, following a joint public appeal with Art Fund supported
by over 8,000 donors
Back cover: North front of the Queen's House, f6025-017

CONTENTS

INTRODUCTION

On 27 April 1937, King George VI, Queen Elizabeth and their elder daughter Princess Elizabeth sailed in the launch *Nore* from Westminster Pier to Greenwich, to open the new National Maritime Museum (NMM). Three weeks before the coronation, it was the first major public event of the King's reign and stage-managed as an opportunity for his subjects to acclaim his unexpected succession to his brother, Edward VIII, whose abdication in 1936 had been a national crisis.

Expectations were not disappointed: the bridges and banks of the Thames were lined with cheering crowds until the King, Queen and Princess disembarked to a naval and civic welcome at the river stairs of the Royal Naval College. A short car journey then took them across the road to the steps of the Queen's House – heart of the newly converted buildings of the Museum, following over 130 years of previous use as the Royal Hospital School. Met there by the King's mother, Queen Mary, who had arrived separately, the royal party was formally welcomed by Earl Stanhope, Chairman of the Museum Trustees, and Professor Geoffrey Callender, its founding Director. On the north terrace of the House, Queen Elizabeth unlocked the door to its Great Hall with a special golden key. The royal party disappeared inside and so began a new phase in the life of a building completed 300 years earlier for very different purposes.

The Queen's House remains the 'jewel in the crown' of the Museum, and the park-and-palace landscape of the Maritime Greenwich World Heritage Site – so inscribed by UNESCO in 1997. It represents no less than the stylistic point of origin of the great classical buildings of Greenwich that surround it, and of classical architecture in Britain more generally. Yet, at the same time, it is also the only major remnant of an earlier landscape – that of the vanished Tudor royal palace at Greenwich, to which it was the last significant addition.

Regrettably, the House's school use from 1807 damaged it more than its previous history, but its story since 1937 has also seen controversy. The 1930s restoration was well done, but its incorporation as part of the NMM initiated a new set of tensions: between changing needs as a place for object and art displays of (at best) limited relation to its largely unknown original uses and furnishing; between its creation for a privileged court circle and the visits it now receives from a broad public to whom the early Stuart mindset is alien and irretrievable; and between the many priorities of a wide-ranging national museum.

The result has been differences of opinion and changes of direction, all within the requirement to use public money for the widest general benefit and subject to a commonly agreed problem. For while no-one disputes that the House is a unique and influential survival from a lost age, and among 'the first and finest classical buildings in England by one of the greatest of British architects', expert opinion has rightly identified a key truth concerning its original intended uses: that 'it was … essentially a secret house which to this day remains an enigma'. (Bold, *Greenwich*, 2000, p. 93)

The early years of the House's designer, Inigo Jones (1573–1652), are equally enigmatic. Almost nothing is known of him until he was 30, except that he was the eldest son of a London cloth-worker of the same name. He probably trained as a joiner, was known by 1603 as a 'picture maker' and, perhaps in that role, may have been part of a court mission to Christian IV of Denmark later that year.

By then, but certainly after 1597, he had already spent some years in Italy and had learnt the language; in 1601 he appears to have bought there his copy of Andrea Palladio's *Quattro libri di architettura*, in which his later marginal jottings show the huge influence it had on his own development as an architect.

His path to eminence, however, was as a designer and producer of court spectacles, especially masques – the elaborate allegorical and audience-participatory entertainments of the reigns of James I and Charles I – the purpose of which was to symbolise and assert the role of the Crown as the earthly embodiment and mirror of divine virtue and order. In many of these, Jones initially, and famously, worked with the playwright Ben Jonson (until they quarrelled), starting in 1605 with *The Masque of Blackness* for James I's queen, Anne of Denmark, who was Christian IV's sister.

At the same time he pursued his personal study of architecture based on Palladio, the published work of Sebastiano Serlio, an Italian translation of Vitruvius, and through a visit to France in 1609. His earliest known architectural designs are from about 1608–09, and from 1610 he was appointed Surveyor to Henry, Prince of Wales, but did little for him before the Prince's early death in 1612.

Shortly afterwards, in April 1613, he gained the reversion as Surveyor of the King's Works, a position he inherited in October 1615 on the death of the incumbent, Simon Basil, and held for 27 years. The period in between, to November 1614, he again spent largely in Italy, accompanying the scholarly Thomas Howard, Earl of Arundel, on an extended tour.

Closely studying classical buildings both ancient and modern, Jones saw Venice, Naples and Rome. Above all he paid attention to the work of Palladio and his circle in Tuscany and the Veneto, concluding, in one of his best-known notebook jottings, that a well-designed building should externally be 'Sollid, proporsionable according to the rulles, masculine and unaffected', but 'inwardly [with] imaginacy set free' in terms of considered ornamentation. In 1616, the Queen's House at Greenwich was to be his first significant opportunity as Surveyor to put these principles into practice.

The Queen's House today

A view of the House from the north with the terrace and 'horseshoe stairs' added in the main part of the second phase of construction from 1632. The bottom of these, and their balustrades, originally faced each other, but were splayed back about 1708 (see p. 128 for detail). The sash windows also replaced Jones's original leaded-glass mullion-and-transom casements at that time. Those on the top floor are the original dimensions; the ground-floor ones originally had higher sills but were then lengthened by cutting these down.

Ancient and modern (pp. 2–3)

The Queen's House today, from the Park, with the domes of the Old Royal Naval College, the Thames and London Docklands behind. When Sir Christopher Wren designed the College (as Greenwich Hospital) in the early 1690s, Queen Mary II specified that it should not block the House's view to the river. The closest distance between the College blocks is exactly the width of the House (115 feet/ 35.4 metres).

BEFORE THE HOUSE

The monumental classicism of the main Greenwich buildings, especially the Old Royal Naval College (originally the Royal Hospital for Seamen, or 'Greenwich Hospital') makes the comparative scale of what preceded them hard to imagine. From the opposite Thames foreshore, around 1600, an observer would have seen the unbroken panorama of the red-brick Palace of Greenwich, rising from a rather lower ground level than the College, with a narrow river walk under its long north frontage. This Tudor palace – the principal London seat of Henry VIII until he built that at Whitehall in the 1530s – was also on a more skewed alignment, since the College stands square-set on levelled-up and, to the east, partly reclaimed land.

A donjon-like square tower, holding the king's private apartments, dominated the river edge, its foundations now well inside the Grand Square a little to the left behind the College water gate. To the far left, the east end of the Chapel, today under the College car park, was also close to the water there, itself then a little further south. The water steps, on the river walk just east of the king's tower, were restricted and the main landing place, near today's Greenwich Pier, was a sloping tidal hard. From there, a route ran south, past the west side of the Palace eventually turning left (east) between it and Greenwich Royal Park. Although the ceremonial approach was by river, any large arrival had to be from that side or from the east; here Henry's 600 x 250-foot tournament ground (or tiltyard) occupied rather more than the eastern side of the present National Maritime Museum site.

The tiltyard boundaries, except to the north, are clear: to the east, what is now Park Row; to the west and parallel, the tiltyard towers and the line of buildings behind, including a 'disguising house' just north-east of the Queen's House. In 1617 this may have hosted the last masque – *Cupid's Banishment* – given at Greenwich for James I's queen, Anne of Denmark, as building of the Queen's House itself began. West of the tiltyard lay the extensive Palace gardens, and both were separated from the Park by the walled Greenwich to Woolwich road; its line was exactly that of the present NMM colonnades.

Access between Palace and Park was by large gates under a residential gatehouse. Stairs either side also allowed this to be used as a royal foot-bridge over the roadway, which may nevertheless have a claim (and Greenwich certainly does) to be where Sir Walter Ralegh ruined his cloak for Elizabeth I to pass dry-shod when he first came to court in 1582. Elizabeth's occasional presence at events in the Park, and her use of the first-floor chamber of the gatehouse to view them, is well recorded. The gatehouse itself appears to have stood on the same ground as the western side of the Queen's House. It had to be demolished for the House to be built.

Greenwich Palace and London from Greenwich, by Anthonis van den Wyngaerde, c.1544

This drawing is one of a pair by Anthonis van den Wyngaerde, the other looking south over the river. The king's private apartments were in the square, donjon-like tower in the centre background, with the former friary church (dissolved in 1534) to the left. Henry VIII's tiltyard, the first added to an English palace in 1515–16, is on the right, flanked by its double towers used for mock assaults. The building immediately behind the towers is the Banqueting House, from which the first of the buildings stretching back to the walled Woolwich road is the tiltyard gallery (which displayed armour) then the 'disguising house' (or theatre). Both banqueting and disguising house were completed early in 1527 for the reception of a French embassy: they saw long use and a great deal is known about them. The Palace gardens lie to their left behind the central gatehouse over the road. The Queen's House replaced this in almost exactly the same position.

Ashmolean Museum, University of Oxford, WA.C.L.G.IV.8b

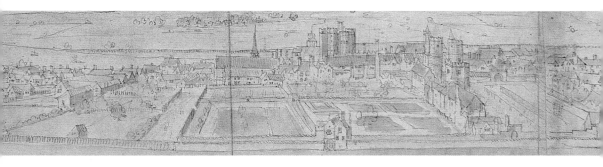

This print is based on an early drawing and other views suggest it compresses the extent of the Palace. It nonetheless shows how the tower holding the king's apartments was built out over the river walk: under the archway there was undoubtedly a private entrance, with access to the steps shown. The Chapel is to the left with the towers of the tiltyard visible far left. Early references often describe the royal complex, and the medieval religious outpost of the Abbey of St Peter at Ghent which preceded it, as being located in 'East Greenwich'. The print title's reference to 'Placentia' (or 'Pleasaunce') is also misleading: this was the royal palace of the mid- to late 1400s (in which Henry VIII was born) but, by 1504, Henry VII had completely redeveloped the site and thereafter it was usually referred to as the Palace of Greenwich.

PAH3294

Greenwich from the Park showing the Tudor palace, c.1615

This painting, by an unknown artist, shows Greenwich from the top of Maze Hill to the south-east. London is in the far distance, with the buildings of Greenwich Palace below by the river, including the tiltyard towers and the 'king's tower'. Aristocratic figures hunt in the Park, which Henry VIII had stocked with deer by 1518. Its early 'pale', or fence, which can clearly be seen, was replaced by an enclosing brick wall from 1619 to 1624. The building on the left is the royal lodge known as Greenwich Castle, which from 1605 to 1614 was held by the Earl of Northampton as Keeper of the Park: the Royal Observatory now stands on its site. In the foreground ladies and gentlemen relax amid grazing sheep, with one couple watching the shepherd's dog dancing to the music of his bagpipes, far left.

BHC1820 (Caird Collection)

A Netherlandish-school painting showing how Greenwich Palace would have appeared to those approaching London by ship up the Thames. Apart from forts downstream it was the first major royal site encountered and therefore ideally placed for official welcomes, such as that of the French ambassadors in 1527, and equally ceremonious departures. Even when important visitors arrived by land from Dover the same applied, since the Dover road probably passed through the Park before it was enclosed and subsequently skirted it across Blackheath, before descending to the river. Although too large and otherwise inaccurate, the building to the left on the hill is most probably the royal lodge called Greenwich Castle.

BHC4168

Henry VII (1457–1509), British school, c.1505

Henry Tudor had mainly non-aristocratic Welsh paternal ancestry, and his father was legitimised on being created 1st Earl of Richmond – a title disputed when he inherited it. His distant claim to the throne was through his mother, Lady Margaret Beaufort, great-great-granddaughter of Edward III. Henry was the last English monarch to seize the Crown in battle, when he defeated and killed Richard III at Bosworth in 1485, thus bringing to an end the 'Wars of the Roses'. As Henry VII he stabilised the country, ruled ably for 23 years, and founded a dynasty that ended with Elizabeth I's death in 1603. His later years were notably rapacious, which among other things enabled him completely to rebuild the old Palace of Placentia, subsequently Greenwich Palace, from about 1498 to 1504. The Queen's House was the last of its significant later adjustments and additions.

BHC2762 (Caird Collection)

Henry is one of the best-known English kings, for both creditable and other reasons. He proved autocratic and ruthless but was also intelligent, very well educated and, in youth, athletic. He was born at Greenwich, as were his daughters Mary I and Elizabeth I, and married both his first and fourth wives there (Katharine of Aragon in 1509 and Anne of Cleves in 1540). From his accession in 1509 Greenwich was Henry's principal and favourite seat until Whitehall Palace was completed in the 1530s; for it was well suited to state and leisure purposes, notably his passions for riding, hunting and jousting. After using open ground in the Park for early jousts, by 1516 he had completed the Greenwich tiltyard, the first in an English palace. Though he welcomed the Emperor Charles V to Greenwich in 1520 and 1522, it was after banqueting and disguising houses were added beside the tiltyard in 1527 that the Palace saw its full ceremonial exploitation. Henry also founded his famous armoury within the Palace complex, one of many ways in which he attempted both to emulate European rivals and impress his status on them.

BHC2763 (Caird Collection)

Edward VI (1537–53), after Hans Holbein, 16th century

Edward was Henry VIII's only son, by his third wife Jane Seymour; she died following his birth. A sickly boy king, from age nine to fifteen a Regency Council governed for him. Henry had made himself head of the Church in England in 1533, instead of the Pope, but maintained Catholic doctrine. It was under Edward that Protestantism took root in England and, as his death approached, he named his (reluctant) cousin Lady Jane Grey as his Protestant heir, excluding his older sisters. This was resisted and nine days after his death the elder, Mary, was proclaimed queen; Jane was executed and Mary's reign was one of savage Catholic reaction. As prince and king, Edward spent more time at Greenwich than at any other palace and died (of tuberculosis) at Old Court, a house a little to the east, on 6 July 1553. This portrait, one of several copies, was formerly owned by the Earls of Guildford at Wroxton Abbey.

BHC2678 (Caird Collection)

Elizabeth was also born at Greenwich, the daughter of Henry VIII's second wife Anne Boleyn – who was arrested for treason as she left the Palace by river in 1536. Elizabeth, a Protestant, succeeded her Catholic half-sister Queen Mary in 1558. Both made great use of Greenwich, especially in summer, and Elizabeth's gardens there were celebrated. Her early use of the gatehouse connecting Palace and Park is also recorded: in July 1559, for example, from its upper chamber, she watched a mock fight in the lower Park by 1,400 men of London's trained bands. Later she saw the *Golden Hind* return from Drake's circumnavigation from the Palace windows, and in 1585 also reluctantly signed the death warrant of Mary Queen of Scots there. Both were among the causes of the Spanish Armada of 1588, against which the Queen's council planned much of the defence at Greenwich. In 2016, following a successful national appeal, Royal Museums Greenwich acquired the 'Armada Portrait' of Elizabeth – probably the defining image of her age – from descendants of Sir Francis Drake (who may have commissioned it). The Queen's House, looking across to the site of the Queen's Lodgings of the old Palace where Elizabeth was born, is now its permanent home. ZBA7719

George Clifford, 3rd Earl of Cumberland (1558–1605), by Nicholas Hilliard, c.1590

This is perhaps the most famous image of Greenwich armour for the tilt – the 'star' suit made for Clifford as Elizabeth I's formal Champion from 1590, in his assumed role as Knight of Pendragon Castle. It does not survive but another of Clifford's does (in New York), and Henry VIII's Greenwich armour is well known. The making of high-status parade and jousting armours, for use and as gifts, was a Continental speciality until Henry began employing European makers in London in 1511. In 1515, with German craftsmen, he founded the 'Almain armoury' at Greenwich Palace. It was near the Observant friary church (where he was baptised and first married) and in 1543, nine years after he dissolved the friary, the church became a new armoury mill. The Greenwich armoury continued, later in more utilitarian work, until 1649. The old Armoury Mill at Lewisham retained that name and continued making plate and, later, firearms until after the defeat of Napoleon in 1815. It was then a silk mill into the 1860s.

MNT0193 (Caird Collection)

THE 'CURIOUS DEVISE' OF INIGO JONES
1616 − c.1638

In 1613 James I gave the manor of Greenwich to his Danish queen, Anne (or Anna), reportedly in apology for losing his temper after she accidentally shot his favourite dog while hunting. She made early improvements in the Queen's Lodgings on the south side of the Palace and had the celebrated garden designer, Salomon de Caus, update Elizabeth I's gardens between them and the Park.

Then, in June 1617, the courtier John Chamberlain reported that 'The Queen…is building somewhat at Greenwich, wch must be finished this sommer, yt is saide to be some curious devise of Inigo Jones, and will cost above 4000li…'. This is an appropriate first reference to the Queen's House, whose design Jones began in October 1616, for 'curious' then meant 'elegant' or 'finished', and 'devise' (device) primarily had the heraldic meaning of an emblem representing its possessor's qualities or aspirations.

The House's other purposes were, first, as a garden retreat for the Queen and her immediate court – which was distinct from the King's and by then rather estranged from it. Second, to replace the Tudor gatehouse as a bridge between Palace and Park, across the walled public road, and as a focal point for activities (e.g. hunting) in the Park. Third, it was perhaps intended to impose a cosmopolitan, 'modern' frontispiece on the late-medieval red-brick palace behind, as seen from the Park and especially the hill above. For in its external design and some internal detail it is the House's southern, sun-facing side that Jones first conceived as the 'front'. This in turn suggests it was intended as a symbolic portal, whose white, classically ordered perfection asserted the Queen's primacy as manorial chatelaine of Greenwich, a role that probably included ceremonious passage between Palace and Park, with the south loggia as a prestigious vantage from which she and important guests could both see and be seen.

Neither Anne nor the House got that far; she died in March 1619, aged 44, but work had stopped in April 1618 with its two separate ground-floor storeys left as brick shells. So they remained, thatched over, until after Charles I in turn vested Greenwich in his French wife, Queen Henrietta Maria, in 1629. Jones then completed the House for her, with final work being done about 1638 and the two-storey ranges linked only by a central bridge. The major addition was the north terrace, built out from the raised foundation vaults on that side. This – and two fairly short-lived iron balconies to the outer pairs of windows above – afforded a better view over the Palace gardens (which the new queen again remodelled); it also marked the start of what came to be the north side's role as the dominant public front, as it is today. Henrietta Maria's likely use of the House was more private than Anne intended, and her interior decoration of it was lavish, including sculpture and specially commissioned paintings, although some of the latter were never delivered. Nevertheless, in 1659, after ten years of Puritan republican rule, memory of the 'house of delight' still lingered as one 'which Queen Mary…so finished and furnished, that it far surpasseth all other of that kind in England'.

Inigo Jones (1573–1652), by William Dobson, c.1642

Images of Jones are consistent with regard to his appearance, dressed in brown, grey or black and wearing a distinctive cap, attire which probably squared his artisan origins with his status as King's Surveyor. Assertions that he or at least his Welsh father were Roman Catholic are unproven and mainly prompted by their unusual first name (a Spanish/Basque version of Ignatius, and thus linked to Loyola, founder of the Jesuits). His baptism and burial suggest otherwise, and a contemporary noted that he was largely 'without religion', itself then unusual. Jones was a fine draughtsman and his masque designs show that he was imaginatively, symbolically and mechanically ingenious: his architecture followed Palladio and his school in being based on the 'magic' relationships of perfect and harmonic number ratios, and often hidden geometry. For the early Stuarts, his work in both areas articulated the neo-Platonic philosophy that kingship was the earthly mirror of divine authority, perfection and order. This late portrait is a life study probably done when Charles I's court was at Oxford early in the Civil War: the talented but short-lived Dobson was the only English painter to approach the quality of Van Dyck, who also painted Jones but died in 1641.

BHC2809 (Caird Collection)

Princess Elizabeth (later the 'Winter Queen' of Bohemia, 1596–1662), aged seven, by Robert Peake, 1603

Elizabeth was the daughter of James I and Anne of Denmark. This portrait was painted in 1603, shortly after James succeeded Elizabeth I and came south from Scotland. Anne, Elizabeth and her brothers Henry (1594–1612), Prince of Wales, and Charles followed. That October Elizabeth was put under the guardianship of Lord Harington at Combe Abbey, Warwickshire. He probably commissioned this portrait, showing her against his park behind; there is a pendant to it of Henry, now in New York. In 1613 Elizabeth married the Elector Palatine Frederick V in London, and they were escorted to his capital at Heidelberg by Thomas Howard, Earl of Arundel, his wife, and a large train including Inigo Jones. Howard was a connoisseur and collector of antique sculpture and Jones, an Italian speaker, was one of the smaller party of four who went on with the Earl and Countess to tour in Italy. This allowed Jones to deepen his study of ancient Roman and Italian Renaissance architecture; he also met Palladio's pupil Vincenzo Scamozzi.

BHC4237 (Acquired with the assistance of The Art Fund and the National Heritage Memorial Fund)

The Arrival of the Elector Palatine at Flushing, 29 April 1613, by Adam Willaerts, 1623

The marriage of Frederick V, Elector of the Rhineland Palatinate, to Princess Elizabeth, daughter of James I, aimed to bolster the Protestant powers in Germany. The couple's initial liking for each other turned into a successful union and they left England from Margate in James I's great flagship *Prince Royal*, named for Henry, Prince of Wales. The princess was attended by a large English party under the Earl of Arundel, including Inigo Jones. It was for Elizabeth, at Heidelberg, that Frederick created famous gardens designed by her former tutor, Salomon de Caus, who also remodelled those at Greenwich for her mother, Anne. In 1619 Frederick's coronation as Protestant King of Bohemia triggered the start of the Thirty Years War. A year later he was defeated by the Catholic Holy Roman Emperor and driven into lifelong exile with Elizabeth, mainly at The Hague, the couple coming to be known as the 'Winter King and Queen' since their reign only lasted a little longer. As a widow, Elizabeth returned to England just before her death in 1662, but her daughter Sophia became the Stuart link to the Hanoverian succession of 1714. Willaerts produced many views of the marriage voyage: this one belonged to Elizabeth's devoted friend, the Earl of Craven, who may have inherited it from her.

BHC4176 (Acquired with the assistance of The Art Fund and the National Heritage Memorial Fund)

James I (1566–1625), by John de Critz, c.1610

James was the only son of Mary, Queen of Scots, who (like Elizabeth I) was Tudor through being a great-granddaughter of Henry VII. Mary and James's father, Henry Stuart, Lord Darnley, were Catholics, unpopular and faced strong Protestant rebellion. Darnley was murdered early in 1567 and Mary quickly married the Earl of Bothwell (her third husband), who was a suspect in this. In July she was imprisoned and deposed by the Protestant rebels and her infant son proclaimed James VI of Scotland, under a regency: she never saw him again and James was raised a Protestant. As distantly Tudor, he also succeeded Elizabeth I as James I of England in 1603. James married Anne of Denmark in 1589 and it proved a sound match, although James's closer relationships were with men. Only three of their children survived, Charles I being the younger son (the elder, Henry, died in 1612). Called 'the wisest fool in Christendom' he was a well-educated thinker, ruthlessly against witchcraft (and smoking) and a notable polemical writer. His *Basilikon Doron* lays out the Stuart conception of rule by divine right, which artists including Rubens, Van Dyck and (in the court masques) Jones and others made physically manifest.

BHC2796 (Caird Collection)

Anne of Denmark (1574–1619), by John de Critz, c.1605

Anne (baptised Anna) was daughter of Frederick II of Denmark and sister of Christian IV, whose court Inigo Jones may have visited in 1599. She was 14 when married to James VI of Scotland by proxy. Storms disrupted her passage there and James personally led a squadron to rescue her from the Norwegian coast – said to be the only romantic thing he ever did. Their union produced many pregnancies and seven children, to 1607, but only three survived infancy. Thereafter they mainly lived apart, though retaining affection and respect. Distancing began early with Anne's interventions in factional Scottish politics: it widened from Prince Henry's birth in 1594, when James made it clear she would have no part in his upbringing. On becoming Queen Consort in England, in 1603, Anne mainly refocused her energies on patronage of the arts, leading a fashionably cultured queen's court that vied with her husband's. Jones's masques specifically praising her (including the first in 1605), and her projected Queen's House at Greenwich, were important elements on her side of this tension: the Banqueting House in Whitehall (1622), for James's masques, is Jones's monument on his, albeit completed after her death. In this portrait she wears pearls inherited from Elizabeth I.

BHC4251

Jones's preliminary response to the unusual brief for a villa built on both sides of a roadway. What is shown – and what was originally built – is an H-plan house whose two wings are linked by a central bridge, here with 'Venetian' windows looking along the road and with Corinthian-column upper-floor porticos to left and right. The drawing also shows deeply recessed outer corners to each range, probably concealing one bay of windows to left and right: in the House as built it is two bays, with a much slighter projection of the central Hall elevation on the north side and that of the Ionic loggia on the south. The plan form is based on the Medici villa at Poggio a Caiano, near Florence, built in the 1480s by Giuliano da Sangallo the Elder, though its two wings are linked by a central *salone*. It is also easy to forget today that the Queen's House was built on sloping ground, south to north, requiring raised foundation vaults on the north side.

By courtesy of the Conway Library, The Courtauld Institute of Art, London, B68/3016

The north front of the Queen's House, c.1635

This drawing by an unknown hand shows the north front as completed to roof level, with the date plaque set in to mark this above the upper central window arch: this reads HENRICA MARIA / REGINA / 1635, stamping the queen's ownership on the work. The lower windows are shown at their original depth. Why the drawing was done is not known.

The left-hand roof turret gave access to the north side of the roof up the 'round stairs' but the right-hand one above a service stair was never added. Light iron balconies to the outer upper windows are also shown and, reportedly, traces of mannerist wall decoration on the façade. The balconies were original features and were replaced in 1694. Their windows

were presumably then full-height, for access, but later reformed to match the others. Unfortunately the drawing is now lost and only known from this record photograph.

Elevation for a chimney-piece and overmantel, by Inigo Jones, 1637

Until recently, an inscription on this 1637 sketch by Jones prompted a long-standing belief that it was a fireplace design for the small cabinet room adjoining the Queen's Withdrawing Room on the upper floor of the house. From 1662 this 'dead-end' cabinet, and the other three similarly placed, were incorporated in the general upper-floor circulation by the insertion of the East and West Bridge Rooms, and the Withdrawing Room became the King's Presence Chamber. Although small-room fireplaces elsewhere in the House are more modest, this one was reconstructed in 1990 in its supposed original position. It has now been recognised that the design is a rejected draft for the Withdrawing Room itself, which was replaced by one similar to just its bottom part (with a low mantel) in order to hang a large painting by Jacob Jordaens above it. Nevertheless, it was of House fire-surrounds like this that a Dutch visitor noted 'the marble leafwork mutilated: the noses of all the faces cut off from love of mischief, committed in the times of Cromwell'.

RIBA Library Photographs Collection, RIBA12964

Charles I and Henrietta Maria, with courtiers, standing on the hill in Greenwich Park, with the Palace and river below: the child holding the Queen's hand is likely to be Charles II (b. 1630). Of the two men talking on the left the one on the right is Endymion Porter who negotiated many of Charles's major art purchases, including the Gonzaga art and antique sculpture collection in 1631: up to ten pieces of this may have been in the Hall of the Queen's House by 1640. The other is sometimes said to be Inigo Jones but is wearing the ribbon of the Order of the Garter which rules him out. The first Earl of Portland is the most recent alternative suggestion, possibly with the Earl of Pembroke (Lord Chamberlain, himself a patron of Jones and later briefly Steward of Greenwich) climbing the hill between Porter and the King. The half-built House can clearly be seen in front of the main Palace. Its single-storey brick ranges are covered with a wooden platform over the road for work to recommence, which mainly occurred from 1632.

The triangular pitch in the centre covers the base of the Centre Bridge arch which was probably structurally complete by 1618 and, with the two wings, then protected against weather by thatch. This was renewed in 1629. The tiltyard can be clearly seen to the right, with the houses of East Greenwich beyond and the river flowing north-east round Greenwich Marshes (today the site of the O2 dome).

Prospect of London and the Thames from above Greenwich, Flemish school, c.1626–28

A Flemish-school painting showing the general landscape from Greenwich towards London. Here the relationship between the House, the tiltyard towers and Greenwich Castle – the residential grace-and-favour lodge on the hill in the Park – is shown from the west (see detail). The House appears as two blocks of one ground-floor storey and it is known from late-1620s accounts, including for repair of two chimney-pieces, that some rooms in it were inhabitable in its half-built state. The houses in front lie along Croom's Hill, the line of which mounts the hill but is as yet lacking a wall; that may make the picture a little earlier since the wall was finished about 1624.

Museum of London, 64.52

This is the first of Hollar's many English topographical etchings. Apart from accurately showing the overall Greenwich Palace complex, it is the first image of the Queen's House as structurally completed in 1635 (the date inscribed on the House's north front). Hollar misses the blind balustrading below the upper windows but the lower ones are shown at original size, with high sills: these were lowered and sashes installed in 1708. The north-east corner roof turret gave access onto the 'leads' from the 'Tulip Stairs' until removed about 1822. The trees of the Queen's Garden lie behind the enclosed road to the left, with its wall on the Park side pierced by Jones's 'fayre great gate', built in 1623–24. The carriage included shows how the south side of the House – then opening directly to the Park – may originally have been intended as a formal entrance approach. On the left Greenwich Castle is shown in its late form. Originally a watchtower and hunting lodge of the 1420s, it had various later residents and embellishments until Parliament garrisoned it to control Greenwich during the Civil War. It later became ruinous and in 1675–76 the Royal Observatory was built on the same foundations.

PAI7662

Queen Henrietta Maria (1609–69), studio of Sir Anthony Van Dyck, c.1638

Henrietta Maria was a daughter of Henri IV of France and sister of Louis XIII, and was married to Charles I just after his accession in 1625. Her devout Catholicism made her unpopular, and she and Charles only became close after the murder of his favourite, the Duke of Buckingham, in 1628. Their sons, later Charles II and James II, were born in 1630 and 1632. 'Queen Mary' was intensely loyal to Charles and they last saw each other in 1643, early in the Civil War, when she escaped to France. Like Anne of Denmark, she was a leader of fashion and the arts: Orazio Gentileschi, lead painter for the Queen's House, came to England with one of her courtiers and she also favoured Guido Reni, though his commission never arrived; sculpture, masques and music were also among her passions. She closely watched the House's completion and decoration, adding the north terrace and apparently making more secluded, intimate use of it than Anne intended. This portrait copies one of a set of three by Van Dyck, apparently from sittings at Greenwich. It was formerly owned by the Earls of Denbigh, the Countess having been the sitter's Mistress of the Robes.

BHC2761 (Caird Collection)

Charles I (1600–49), by Daniel Mytens the Elder, 1629

Charles's accession, in 1625, poses one of the 'what ifs' of British history; for he was James I's younger son, and his much-praised elder brother Henry, Prince of Wales – who died of typhoid in 1612 – had shown signs of being more able. As a patron of the arts Charles was pre-eminent among British monarchs, only George IV approaching his discernment as a collector; as king, however, he combined an inflexible conception of his duty as God's appointed ruler with characteristic Stuart stubbornness. The result was the collapse of the uneasy balance between Crown and Parliament, a seven-year civil war and his execution in January 1649. In 1688 similar traits led to the overthrow of his younger son, James II. Charles and Henrietta Maria were last briefly at Greenwich Palace in September 1642, before she took their daughter Mary to Holland to marry the Prince of Orange, and raise money for the royal cause. After his death the art works at Greenwich, including those in the Queen's House, were sold off from September 1649. This is one of many such portraits by Mytens, who was Charles's court painter from 1625 but who was rapidly eclipsed by Van Dyck from 1632.

BHC4228

The Hall is nominally a 40-foot cube but not precisely, owing to construction adjustments. The floor of white Bardiglio (Italian) and black Belgian marble mirrors the ceiling compartments above and was laid by Gabriel Stacey in 1636–37, working under Nicholas Stone, Charles I's Master Mason. The ceiling and gallery woodwork still show Jones's original paint scheme of white and gold – the colours of France – for Henrietta Maria: the white has degraded to green under the 24 later paint layers stripped off in the 1930s. Up to ten antique marble statues on carved wooden bases were originally placed here and large pictures (possibly over hangings) on the walls, and on the gallery above. In 2016, ahead of the 400th anniversary of its construction in 1617, the house underwent significant refurbishment, and the Great Hall was improved by new lighting and repainting, including an original artwork for the ceiling by Richard Wright.

L2150-004

The 'round stairs' or 'Tulip Stairs'

This is the earliest centrally unsupported spiral stair in England, on the Italian Renaissance model. Its position, off the corner of the Hall, and the lack of resting points below the upper floor, show this was primarily conceived as a descending flight. Those coming across the Centre Bridge appear dramatically on the gallery through an imposing doorway with the Royal Arms above, and can also 'make an entrance' into the Hall from the bottom. Above gallery level, there are two small landings at 15-step intervals which aid ascent to a larger one at the top. This originally gave access to the leads of the roof for views over the Palace and along the river, via a wooden rotunda that was removed in about 1822. The stair has strength as well as elegance, based on compression, its precisely cut stone treads locking into each other and the enclosing wall. The basement extension only dates from the 19th century. The wrought-iron rail design was first called 'tulips' in a repair account of 1694, but they are probably lilies, the royal flower of France, in compliment to Henrietta Maria. They may also be an addition of the 1670s between previously plain upright bars.

S0023-004

This series of nine paintings is by the Florentine artist Orazio Gentileschi (1563–1639), who in 1626 followed Henrietta Maria to England and became one of her favoured artists. Jones probably based the Venetian compartmented ceiling on Palladio's Villa Barbaro, at Maser, and the thematic programme reflects the image of benign and civilised rule that the Caroline court wished to project. The House also held other paintings by Gentileschi and one (now lost) by his daughter Artemisia; she probably helped her father to finish the ceiling and oversaw its installation at the time of his death. It was reserved to the State after Charles's execution, when the House was stripped of art works, then possibly stored and replaced in 1661. Finally removed in 1708, Queen Anne gave it to her favourite, Sarah Churchill, Duchess of Marlborough, who had it adjusted to fit the hall ceiling of Marlborough House, London, in 1711. This image shows the 'Scanachrome' copy installed in 1989, a computer-aided technique that also enabled the side panels holding paired figures to be restretched to original length and other smaller 'restorations'. It is still in place but covered by a removable surface.

D5008-1

The Hall ceiling today

Until 1969 the compartments of the Hall ceiling remained empty and were simply painted white. In that year, the Museum installed a large early 18th-century circular oil painting of 'The Triumph of Peace', which was attributed to Sir James Thornhill (who decorated the Painted Hall of Greenwich Hospital). During the 1980s restoration of the House it was removed and resold on the grounds of not being sufficiently contemporary with the building, and in the process the painter was identified as Louis Chéron (1660–1725), a French artist who worked in England from around 1690 to his death and was a collaborator with Thornhill in some work. In 2016, the first original new artwork for the Hall's ceiling since the 1630s was commissioned from Turner Prize-winning artist Richard Wright. An untitled abstract work, this consists of a pattern of repeating decorative motifs drawn from the design of the Tulip Stairs, filling the ceiling panels and extending down the upper part of the walls. Each element is individually applied in 23-carat gold leaf.

L9842-026 and L9842-036

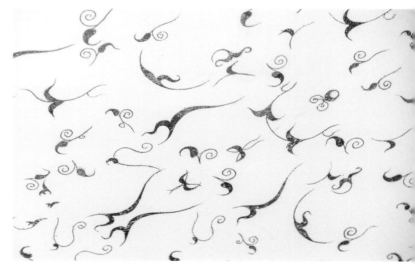

This is a detail from a survey of June 1693 in manuscript and watercolour. To the right the House bridges the road with the original tripartite arch and balcony of its West Bridge Room clearly shown, and with Jones's Park gate at the end of the 'New Road'. The Queen's Garden is still in place, with square beds or lawns and walks (see also pp. 9, 79). The buildings in the tiltyard – then a firework-testing ground – are also clearly described in a numbered key: 'The firemaster's house and garden'

(6); 'Admiral Davis's Stable' (7); 'The Long Storehouse' (8); 'The Laboratory' (9); 'The Turret' - the one surviving tiltyard tower (10); and 'the Kitchen' (11). Top left, by the river, 'the ruines of the old Chappell' (2) lie above 'The Works' – the site of the former Palace – with the ground plan of the eastern range of what is now the King Charles Court of the Old Royal Naval College below. Further numbers identify houses, gardens and stables of 'officers belonging to ye Works' and others, and 'B' is 'the Elm Nursery' for the

Park. The 'Dwarf Orchard' above it along Park Vista still exists. The fenced enclosure south (right) of the House is probably to exclude deer. A further marginal detail of 'The South Side of the Queen's house' is not precise, giving the loggia only three freestanding columns, not four, and omitting the east balcony. It nonetheless shows well the original window patterns and dimensions, the wall on the east side and roof details.

The National Archives, MR/329(1)

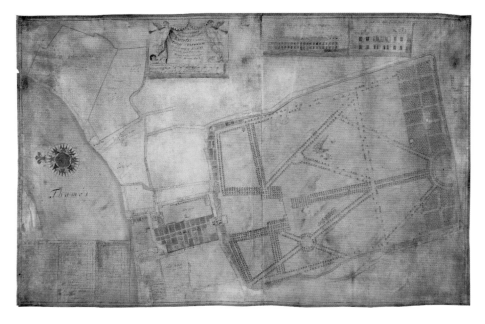

The House from the north-west today

A photograph which shows how, whatever Jones's original intention, the north side has become the public front of the House. This started with the addition of the north terrace and, as far as visual representations of the whole Greenwich site are concerned, was complete by the mid-18th century. By that time, most formal perspectives of Greenwich Hospital are from the north, often from an imaginarily elevated position, and have the House in the background. The addition of the early-19th-century colonnades and flanking wings then produced a three-sided north-facing arena with the House as its focus. This fitted well with the Hospital, and coincidentally also echoes Wren's rejected first plan for that, but 'one block' south. To the man (literally) in the street, however, the reversal would only have become fully clear after all surrounding walls to both sides were changed to railings in the early 1860s. Until then the House could really only be seen from the Park and only had a clear visual relationship to the Hospital buildings on the river side when seen from the hill above, by the Observatory.

L0517

The original exterior north door to the undercroft, c.1617

Until the 1630s this was the external door into the vaults of the House's raised north-side foundations, required by the river-ward slope of the ground. There is no evidence that the vaults were otherwise accessible until an internal service stair was extended downwards off the south-west corner of the Hall, about 1662. They had windows on all sides, however, light being admitted to the sub-ground ones on the roadway front and to east and west by horizontal gratings, so may have been used for storage. There is a similar Jones sketch dated 1635 for the replacement external door, at the north end of the corridor formed when the terrace was added. (The one now between its 'horseshoe stairs' seems to be 18th-century.) Before the 1635 terrace addition, how people were intended to reach the Hall entrance is not known. Jones may have envisaged a narrower access terrace on built-up ground, reached from each side, bridging the basement door and also requiring gratings to admit light to the basement north windows.

L5008

Henrietta Maria's enjoyment of her House was brief. In 1643, as the Civil War developed, she fled to France. After Charles I's defeat and execution in 1649, Parliament sold 'the late King's goods' including the art works from Greenwich. The old Palace fell into decay but the House was reserved for government use, though it suffered some neglect and vandalism. By 1648 Bulstrode Whitelocke, a lawyer, diplomat and joint Keeper of the Parliamentary Great Seal, was Steward of Greenwich but in February 1649 exchanged this role with the Earl of Pembroke for a similar one in Windsor forest. Whitelocke had personal Greenwich links, but John Evelyn's assertion in a diary entry of March 1652 that he then held the House is misleading. Cromwell briefly considered occupation, late in 1653, but this went no further and its only official use was for the lying in state of two Parliamentary Generals at Sea: Richard Deane in 1653, killed in the First Anglo-Dutch War (which saw prisoners detained in the old Palace) and the great Robert Blake in 1657, after he died off Portsmouth on his return from victory against the Spanish.

The Restoration in 1660 brought renewed attention to the House, Charles II recognising the potential of Greenwich for grandiose redevelopment on the river highway into London. August 1661 saw work start on the addition of the House's East and West Bridge Rooms. Exactly who designed them is unclear, but 'draughts' were prepared by William de Keyser which gave the upper floor today's fully connected square plan, with King's Side and Queen's Side apartments (to east and west), progressing from 'public' Presence Chambers on the north front round to 'private' bedchambers overlooking the Park. The Bridge Rooms originally had balconies looking east and west along the road and retain their fine moulded ceilings by Charles II's Master Plasterer, John Grove. On the Queen's Side, what had originally been Henrietta Maria's bedchamber – the only room with painted ceiling decoration – became the Queen's Presence Chamber, while the large south-east and south-west rooms were partitioned as bedchambers with adjoining closets. The Earl of St Alban, who became Keeper of the Palace site in April 1662, may have played a part in these changes, and the Queen's (south-west) bedroom closet was probably first used as a Catholic chapel by Henrietta Maria as Queen Dowager. She landed from France and resumed occupation in July, while Somerset House was adapted for her. Perhaps hastened by sad memories, her move there in September (before Somerset House was complete) ended the history of Greenwich as a 'royal seat': December saw a Russian embassy lodged in the House, a diplomatic use that was occasionally repeated into the 1690s.

Overall, it is ironic that as the last significant addition to the Palace of Greenwich, and the part least used for its original purposes, the House's adaptability made it the element that survived. It remained vested in successive queens, but thereafter saw only occasional royal visits or overnight stays, usually related to Greenwich's role as the normal point of important arrivals and departures by royal yacht for the Continent.

This is the only room in the House with a painted ceiling, decorated in the Italian mannerist style. Research in 2016 has now suggested the artist is Edward Pearce senior. Henrietta Maria commissioned a 'Bacchus and Ariadne' for the centre from Guido Reni, one of her favourite artists, but it did not arrive and (though recorded in a print) was destroyed in France about 1650. A pre-existing 'Daedalus and Icarus' by Giulio Romano replaced it about 1640, when Richard Dirgin carved a frame among several others for the room; this was rated the most valuable work in the House in 1649, other than the Gentileschi Hall ceiling works, and though reserved from sale it disappeared at some point during the Commonwealth. How the gap was filled is unclear until the present canvas of 'Aurora dispersing the shades of Night' arrived. When and how it was acquired are uncertain, as is the identity of the artist and whether it was painted in the late 17th or early 18th century. The corners of the painted surround bear Latin mottoes translating as 'Mutual fruitfulness/ the hope of the state/ burns forever/ with pure fragrance'. The inscription HENRICA MARIA REGINA appears in the coving over the fire, with the Royal Arms opposite.

D4949

The Queen's Bedchamber as a Presence Chamber of about 1670

The same room photographed in the 1990s, in the House's 'refurnished' presentation of that time, as the Queen's Presence Chamber, about 1670. It holds a 'chair of estate' behind which original tapestries representing the story of Theodosius of Byzantium and the Apple hang against plain red silk wall hangings. The fireplace is a cast replica of a 17th-century one at nearby Charlton House (built by Sir Adam Newton, tutor to James I's elder son Henry, Prince of Wales), which may itself have been removed from the Queen's House, though this is uncertain. The 17th-century paintings are a 'Battle of Actium' by Lorenzo Castro, and Henri Gascars' portrait of James, Duke of York (James II), in Roman armour as Lord High Admiral (to 1673). Gascars, appropriately, was a French court painter who worked for the Catholic clique – of which James was leader – in the post-Restoration English court. The portrait remained in the Royal Collection until given to Greenwich Hospital by William IV.

National Monuments Record, bb96/00693

The 1660s Queen's Bedchamber reconstructed

A 1990 view of the south-west corner room on the top floor. The silk wall hangings, wood-panel dadoes on the lower walls, the dividing rail and the marbled paint effects were part of the attempt to reconstruct a 1670s environment. The room was also repartitioned as it was in the 1660s, which is why the fire appears off-centre.

This formed a Queen's Closet in the smaller part adjacent to the south loggia, and Henrietta Maria probably briefly used this as a place for prayer, with discreet access for a priest up the South Stairs (which usefully service several rooms on the south side this way). Privacy for the great at this time was a very relative

term, even in a bedchamber: apart from the queen, only body servants and intimate relatives, friends or favourites would be allowed within the rail. For the paintings over the fire and to the right, see p. 25 and p. 26.

D4944-005

'Psyche Consoled by Pan', by Jacob Jordaens, 1640

A preliminary drawing for the first picture dispatched by Jacob Jordaens of Antwerp in a series of 22, commissioned for the Queen's Withdrawing Room from 1639 (see p. 55). The detailed brief from Jones must have been agreed with the Queen, negotiations were complex and Jordaens was not told the purpose, in order to keep the price down. The chosen theme, the legend of Cupid and Psyche (from Apuleius), was one central to the Stuart myth of Charles and Henrietta Maria as a perfect union, divinely appointed to rule an ideal state. The description it includes of Psyche's exquisitely decorated magic palace undoubtedly related to the Queen's conception of her 'house of delight'. Room-layout diagrams now in the city archive, Antwerp, show this canvas was on the upper east wall. It arrived in the summer of 1640 but only eight of the others definitely came, by mid-1641. All were thought lost until this one re-emerged in France in the 1990s. It was briefly rehung in the room when the Museum considered purchase, but its condition and cost made this impractical.

Museum Plantin-Moretus/Prentenkabinet, Antwerp, OT 163

The Queen's Withdrawing Room (1630s), later King's Presence Chamber, as reconstructed today

The north-east corner room on the top floor looking towards the Hall. This has the most elaborate wood-carving in the House and would have been the most richly decorated space, with a series of 22 paintings by Jacob Jordaens representing the legend of Cupid and Psyche on its walls and ceiling. Gilded blue seems to have been the original colour of the carved work, including the removable wall panels (of which two are early and the others modern reproductions). The carving detail includes festoons of fruit and flowers, masks, fleurs-de-lys – for Henrietta Maria – and her and Charles's CR/HM intertwined monogram. While Jordaens' paintings were on order – and not all came – other works were in the room. They included Orazio Gentileschi's 'Lot and his Daughters', later moved to the Hall; his daughter Artemisia's 'Tarquin and Lucretia', works by Van Dyck and Giulio Romano, and others in the Gonzaga collection purchased from Mantua, including Tintoretto's 'The Muses'. Though sold in 1649, Charles II retrieved the last at his Restoration. From 1662 the room became the King's Presence Chamber, though never actively used as such. The fire surround is a late-18th-century example, probably brought into the House from Greenwich Hospital and moved here in the 1980s.

D5012-001

Detail of one of the royal monograms carved in the ceiling of the Queen's Withdrawing Room, 1630s

This represents the conjoined initials of the King and Queen (*Carolus Rex / Henrica Maria Regina*) which also appear, painted, in the original Queen's Bedchamber. The carving of the Withdrawing Room and Hall seems to have been done by Thomas James, Richard Dirgin (or Durkin) and two other unnamed men, who worked on the House for about 18 months from mid-1635. About the end of 1636 James and Dirgin were impressed by the Navy's carver John Christmas, 'out of the Queen's Majesty's

work at Greenwich' to assist in the decoration of Charles I's great warship *Sovereign of the Seas* at Woolwich Dockyard, where she was launched in 1637. In January 1637 Jones ordered James to other work in Somerset House and, on his non-appearance at Woolwich, Christmas had him and (apparently) Dirgin committed to the Marshalsea prison, with stiff bail set at £40. Jones came to their aid and, though the outcome is unclear, obtained the release of other men in similar cases.

L4917-002

Cash accounts show that the road
under the House was diverted
round the Park side to erect the
scaffolding to build the East and
West Bridge Rooms in 1661–62.
Charles II vested the House in
his queen, Catherine of Braganza,
in 1670, but improvements
were initially to upgrade it
for Henrietta Maria, as Queen
Dowager. These were probably
overdue. The Greenwich under-
housekeeper, Uriah Babington,
had managed to stay in charge
since 1634 and his appointment
was renewed in 1660; but Zachary
Plott, a former Greenwich
servant, then told Charles that 'the
Queen Mother's buildings…are
now employed to Entertain rude
and debauched persons to drink
and revel on Sabbath days'. The
(differing) fine plaster ceilings of
the Bridge Rooms are by Charles's
Master Plasterer, John Grove, and
the new top-floor plan allowed
division into a King's Side (east)
and Queen's Side (west). The
former was never used as such, but
the East Bridge became its Privy
Chamber. The inner arches of
both Bridges are now single spans,
like the Centre Bridge. Originally
they had central arches on pillars,
with lower footway side-openings
under guardrooms above. The
outer pillars are now incorporated
in the House walls, but the rest

were removed in the 18th century
and rooms built under the 1660s
Bridges, after the roadway was
moved north.

1933

Greenwich and London from One Tree Hill, by Johannes Vorsterman, c.1680

The best view from this vantage point just after completion of Flamsteed House (1675–76), the original Royal Observatory building, on the footings of Greenwich Castle. Beyond the lower Park, laid out to André Le Nôtre's 1660s design, fine houses run down Croom's Hill to Greenwich itself, with the pre-1710 Church of St Alfege. The Queen's House, still with its original windows, now has its 1660s Bridge Rooms of which the short-lived balcony of the eastern one projects over the road below.

The turret onto the roof from the 'round stairs' allowed enjoyment of a wide view up and down the river at this time over the remains of the old Palace. One of the ruined tiltyard towers is obvious and less so (far right on the river edge) the old Chapel: both of these lasted into the late 1690s. The new element on the site is the first part of Charles II's palace project, built by Denham and Webb in the 1660s. It remained a windowless shell until incorporated as the east front of Wren's King Charles Court of Greenwich Hospital

from 1696. The painting makes a pair with one of Windsor Castle, both presented to the Hospital in 1830. Another version by Vorsterman shows a carriage arrival or departure at the House's door to the Park, in line with the south façade's designed role as the original formal 'front' of the building.

BHC1808 (Greenwich Hospital Collection)

The Orangery overlooking the Park

This fine transverse space, beneath the upper loggia, is the same width as the Hall on the north side of the House. It has long been called 'The Orangery' but only because of its form and Henrietta Maria's known interest in such cultivation: it was never used as such. Jones undoubtedly designed it as a transitional space – a vestibule for entry from or exit to the Park consistent with the House's use as a hunting lodge. Its inner wall (left) has the same exterior-form windows as those originally in the House's ground-floor outer walls. These light further inner spaces behind. It also once had a 12-foot-high pair of central 'air-lock' doors, of which hinge pintles remain, opening inwards to the central south corridor. It is easy to imagine riders arriving from the Park, dismounting outside the open exterior door and entering for refreshments; or leaving their horses with grooms and using the House in its bridge function and crossing privately to the Palace side. In the early 18th century the South-East Parlour beyond the far door was, first, a kitchen and later a dining room for the Governor of Greenwich Hospital.

L5021-002

This elegant stairway is the only vertical access on the south side. If, as has been suggested, the House was originally conceived as a new visual frontispiece and privileged entry to the Palace from the Park, these were 'ascending' stairs. Their two landings suggest this, not least for ladies in heavy gowns. Jones's original balustrade design is unknown and, by the 1930s, there was just a utilitarian early 19th-century railing: the present rococo one was installed in 1936 from Pembroke House, Whitehall (1724), when this was demolished to build the new Ministry of Defence. Jones's supporter, the Earl of Pembroke, was briefly Steward of Greenwich in 1649–50 under the Commonwealth, a period in which the House suffered some vandalism: this example of fine, if slightly off-period, recycling from his family's later London home is architecturally appropriate compensation. The clock is a complex and celebrated astronomical one of about 1705 by Edward Cockey of Warminster.

L5009-007

Edward Montagu, 1st Earl of Sandwich, by Sir Peter Lely, 1666

Montagu was a Parliamentary soldier in the Civil War but went on to be a successful naval commander. He became one of the Generals at Sea in 1656, but by 1660 had joined the group who engineered the Restoration of Charles II. In May that year, when he commanded the squadron that brought Charles back from Dutch exile, he was accompanied by his young kinsman and secretary, Samuel Pepys, and told him that they would 'rise together' thereafter, as they did. In July he became Earl of Sandwich and received many other honours from Charles but, as a vice-admiral, was killed at the Battle of Solebay against the Dutch in 1672. This portrait is one of a famous series called the 'Flagmen of Lowestoft'. They were painted for Charles's brother James who, as Lord High Admiral, led the fleet to victory over the Dutch at the Battle of Lowestoft in 1665 and ordered portraits of a dozen of his senior commanders 'to hang in his chamber'. George IV gave most of them to the Naval Gallery at Greenwich Hospital in 1824; some or all now usually hang in the Queen's House.

BHC3007 (Greenwich Hospital Collection)

After their father's execution in 1649, Charles and his younger brothers, James and Henry, lived in exile in France, the Dutch Republic and Germany. His attempt to retake England from Parliament was defeated in 1651 but Cromwell's death, and the absence of an effective successor, brought about his Restoration in 1660. He introduced the taste for both marine painting and yachting from Holland, strongly supported the Navy and, in two seaborne wars with the Dutch, advanced British maritime dominance. Charles granted the Queen's House to his wife, Catherine of Braganza, in 1670, and in July 1662 both welcomed his mother (Henrietta Maria) at Greenwich on her return to England. He had already altered the House for her short-term residence, continued to improve the Park and, in 1675, built his Royal Observatory there. In March 1664, at Greenwich, Samuel Pepys saw 'the foundacion laying of a very great house for the King, which will cost a great deal of money' and, though this had stalled by 1669, the single, unfinished wing was later incorporated into Wren's Greenwich Hospital. In June 1666 Pepys also saw Charles and James go up into Greenwich Park to hear the gunfire of the Four Days Battle with the Dutch, borne in on the east wind.

MNT0188 (Caird Collection)

Richard Deane (1610–53), General at Sea, by Robert Walker, c.1653

Deane was a Gloucestershire Puritan who appears to have had some early sea-training but was a successful Parliamentary soldier in the Civil War. He was a 'regicide' (one of the signatories of Charles I's death sentence) and in 1649, with Robert Blake and Edward Popham, became one of the first three Parliamentary Generals at Sea. Fighting in the First Anglo-Dutch War (1651–54), he was killed at the Battle of the Gabbard on 1 June 1653. His body lay in state in the Great Hall of the Queen's House before burial in Westminster Abbey, though dug up and desecrated at the Restoration. Robert Walker painted many of the Parliamentary leaders, often using Van Dyck portraits as models. This is based on Van Dyck's first portrait of Algernon Percy, Earl of Northumberland, as Charles I's Lord Admiral, which Walker must have known since it was not engraved.
BHC2646

Robert Blake (1599–1657), General at Sea, by Samuel Cooper, c.1650

Blake was one of a family of 13 children from Bridgwater, Somerset. He was educated at Oxford to 1625, then became a merchant and, in 1640, MP for Bridgwater. Despite having no previous military experience he proved an effective Parliamentary soldier in the Civil War and became one of the first three Generals at Sea in 1649. In this area too he proved extraordinarily good as a fighting commander against the Royalists, then the Dutch and Spanish. He also effected important naval reforms, and until the rise of Nelson was rated with Drake as Britain's greatest sea hero. In 1657, during the Anglo-Spanish War, he died off Portsmouth on his return from defeating a Spanish fleet off Santa Cruz de Tenerife. Like Deane, he lay in state in the Queen's House before burial in Westminster Abbey, but (again) Charles II had his body dug up in 1661: it was reburied in a common pit. This miniature previously belonged to the banker J. P. Morgan. It is the only original contemporary portrait of Blake now located, with a very old attribution to Cooper, though if so it is not in his best style.

MNT0192 (Caird Collection)

The van de Veldes, father and son, were renowned Dutch marine painters, known for recording the triumphs of the Dutch navy up to around 1670. Willem the Elder (1611–93) was a draughtsman, though he also painted, and sailed officially with their fleet to witness its sea actions. Willem the Younger, originally his father's pupil, was also a natural draughtsman and a better painter. Both came to England in 1672/3 in response to a general invitation to Dutch artists from Charles II, who gave them use of the South-West Parlour in the Queen's House as a studio and paid each £100 a year, the father for drawing 'sea fights' and the son for 'putting the said Draughts into colours'. They did other subjects and for other patrons as well, and the Younger also later sailed with the British fleet. Their work, above all, established the taste for marine painting in England. They first lived in East Lane, Greenwich (now Feathers Place and Eastney Street; see p. 45) and seemed to have used the House until moving to Westminster, probably just before the Elder's death. The old identification of this oil-on-copper miniature is based on appearance, but a further clue is the inclusion of a building resembling the Royal Observatory on the right.

MNT0131

An artist in his studio, by Michiel van Musscher, c.1665

This portrait of a young artist, in a Dutch interior with some spatial similarity to the Queen's House, is traditionally identified as Willem van de Velde the Younger. The reasons are primarily his appearance and the presence in the foreground of what are meant to be ship studies by his father, Willem the Elder. The problem is the subject he is painting: apparently a landscape with a large tower, with another landscape behind, though the small paintings high on the right wall include marine subjects. The landscapes suggest that the sitter is more likely to be Willem's short-lived younger brother Adriaen (1636–72), who was a good landscape and animal painter. Unsurprisingly, they may also have looked similar. In either case, the young artist shown is not using the ship drawings in the foreground; they simply identify and pay compliment to Willem the Elder, as the parent of such talent.

Sammlungen des Fürsten von und zu Liechtenstein, Vaduz-Wien, GEO3297

The Mary, *yacht, arriving with Princess Mary at Gravesend in a fresh breeze, 12 February 1689, by Willem van de Velde the Younger,* c.1689

James II succeeded his elder brother, Charles II, in 1685, as an open Roman Catholic. Though initially tolerated, this and the inept policies he pursued as a result soon turned opinion against him. Then, in June 1688, his second wife produced a Catholic male heir (James, later the 'Old Pretender') and a Protestant cabal invited his Dutch son-in-law, Willem of Orange, to invade England and depose him. Willem

and his army were welcomed at Torbay in November, marched with barely a shot fired to London and James fled to France. Van de Velde's painting records the arrival of Willem's wife Mary – James's Protestant elder daughter. Her right of succession was the basis of the so-called 'Glorious Revolution' and she and Willem were crowned joint monarchs in 1689 as William III and Mary II – the only such example in modern

British history. The picture was probably painted in the Queen's House South-West Parlour and it is to Mary that the House owes its view to and from the Thames, which it did not originally have. As the prime champion of the building of Greenwich Hospital, she ordered Wren to preserve this 'visto' in its design, shortly before her death from smallpox in 1694, aged 37.

BHC0328 (Caird Collection)

In 1672 Charles II visited ships
of the fleet that were being
refitted in the Thames following
the Battle of Solebay that May,
where his brother James, Duke
of York, commanded the fleet.
The visit here is likely to be that
of 6 June (OS) as Charles and
James go aboard his flagship
Prince (flying the royal standard)
from the yachts *Cleveland* and
Anne, to hold a Council of War.
James was then still Lord High
Admiral (to 1673) and probably
suggested the subject. The picture
was probably painted in the
Queen's House shortly afterwards
where (as recounted by George
Vertue about 1715) two Admiralty
commissioners admired it and said
that they would 'beg it of the King
& cutt it in Two & each take a
part'. After they left van de Velde
took it off the stretcher and rolled
it up. He got it out again many
years later, retouched it and
sold it privately for £130. This
was probably in 1696 after he
moved into London, since it
bears that date.

BHC0299 (Caird Collection)

One of a set of Mortlake tapestry hangings depicting the Battle of Solebay (Southwold Bay) on the Suffolk coast, between the Dutch and Anglo-French fleets on 28 May 1672 (OS). De Ruyter was the senior Dutch commander; James, Duke of York, in the *Prince*, was in overall allied command,the last time a future British king led a fleet in battle; and the Comte d'Estrées led the French (then allied with Britain). The design here shows the burning of the *Royal James*, flagship of the Earl of Sandwich, which was decimated by gunfire and set alight by a fireship. Sandwich refused to abandon her and drowned, though his body was later washed up and identified by the Garter star on his breast. This is one of a set of six, the first three now being in the Royal Collection. The van de Veldes were allowed space to lay out the large patterns for them on the upper floor of the House.

TXT0106

Apart from the Observatory replacing Greenwich Castle in 1675–76, this view would be recognisable to anyone standing here around 1670, though time has softened the tree-lined architrave of André Le Nôtre's artificially levelled parterre. It has also destroyed the 'Giant Steps', with which the north face of the hill was terraced at the same time. The Ionic loggia itself is the principal external feature of the House. Though there were ground-floor examples – to which the Orangery has functional parallels – this is the earliest first-floor one known in England, following a 1615 note Jones made in his copy of Palladio that such 'a frontispiece in the midest' was a house's finest ornament. It is also an inspiring space from which to view the Park, and be seen from it. This was undoubtedly its royal purpose, given that the Park only became 'public' in modern terms in the early 19th century; in the 1600s it was used solely by those close to the court. It also relates to queenly hunting by following Serlio's pre-scription of Ionic columns in build-ings for 'matrons', and Vitruvius's of the Ionic order for those dedicated to Diana, goddess of the hunt. The balustrades are 1930s reconstruc-tions, following an early-18th-century drawing by John James.

L5020

John Flamsteed (1646–1719), first Astronomer Royal, after Thomas Gibson, 1721

The Revd John Flamsteed was born near Derby and first made his name locally as an astronomer. In 1670 in London he met Jonas Moore, Surveyor of the Ordnance, who became both his most important early patron and in 1675 the builder of the Royal Observatory at Greenwich, to designs by Wren, then King's Surveyor as Inigo Jones had been. Wren's Observatory (Flamsteed House, right) may consciously compliment Jones, since its north side echoes details of the latter's work on Old St Paul's. With Moore's backing Flamsteed became Charles II's first 'astronomical observator' in 1675, charged 'to applye himselfe… to the rectifieing the Tables of the motions of the Heavens, and the places of the fixed stars, so as to find out the so much desired Longitude of places for the perfecteing the Art of Navigation'. Construction of the Observatory on the old footings of Greenwich Castle began in August and Flamsteed moved in in July 1676. In between he had lodgings in the Queen's House to be in touch with the work, and made observations from there. For the next 43 years, he lived looking down over it. This print reproduces a portrait of 1712, when he was 66.

PAD2713, L4871-001

The Royal Observatory from Croom's Hill, British school, c.1696

This picture includes a detail (below) of the old Palace site in the late 1690s. The Queen's House has lost its east balcony but still has the road running beneath it and its original windows. Jones's classical Park gate is also well shown at the angle with the 'New Road', which heads north towards the Greenwich landing place. The top of the remaining tiltyard tower (the 'turret') just projects above the House. Immediately to the left, to the north of the tiltyard, buildings of the former Palace include official residences and probably the east end of the old Chapel, marked as ruinous in the 1693 survey (p. 45). This was only finally cleared away in 1699. The tiltyard itself had been a firework-testing ground since the 1680s, and the next building along the wall to the right of the House was its 'laboratory'. By 1710 the yard was a strawberry field. Further left of the House, across the apparently bare Queen's Garden, Charles II's windowless new 'King's House' lies behind the east-west wall that by 1699 would mark the line of Romney Road. In the distance, where the river turns east towards Woolwich, ships can be seen under construction at Blackwall, where the private merchant shipyard became the world's largest by the late 1700s. It remained a ship-repair and engineering site until 1987.

BHC1812

GRACE AND FAVOUR
1663–1805

In 1663 Charles II began to enlarge the House with corner pavilions; foundations were dug for the southern pair but (fortunately) soon backfilled. His remodelling of the Park behind proceeded, however, to a design by André Le Nôtre, creator of the gardens of Versailles for Louis XIV. Time has softened Le Nôtre's landscaped parterre to the south, but his overall Park layout of tree avenues remains largely intact. Shortly afterwards (1663–72) Jones's pupil John Webb put up the unfinished shell of a new 'King's House' on the Palace site, only used as a gunpowder store until incorporated from 1696 in the King Charles Court of the Royal Hospital for Seamen (now the Old Royal Naval College). The Queen's House slipped into new 'grace-and-favour' uses. One of Charles II's mistresses, Jane Middleton, lodged there, and for about 20 years from 1672/3 the Willem van de Veldes, the Dutch father and son who introduced marine painting to England under Charles II's patronage, had their studio in the South-West Parlour. In 1675–76, the first Astronomer Royal, John Flamsteed, lived in and observed from the House while his new Observatory rose on the hill above. The Marquis de Ruvigny, a French Huguenot refugee, was a longer-term tenant by 1686, sharing quarters for a time with another French exile, the traveller Sir John Chardin, by then jeweller to the English court: one room was used as a Huguenot chapel with services in French for others living locally.

From 1690 the House was attached to the new post of Ranger of Greenwich Park which in 1697 passed to Henry, Earl of Romney. He quickly moved the road under the House north, to its present position, after which it became possible to insert new rooms linking the two halves at ground level. The first was built (apparently by Romney) under the Centre Bridge before 1710, when the House became residence of the Governor of the Hospital. For over 20 years, as the Hospital slowly went up on the Palace site (1696–1751), the Governor also doubled as Ranger. Important changes of 1708 were removal of the Hall ceiling paintings and replacement of the original casement windows in the outer-facing walls with sashes, lengthened at ground level.

By this time the South-East Parlour was a kitchen but in 1723 became the Governor's dining room, and still has the fireplace that was installed then. In 1729 the Hospital lost hope of gaining the House permanently, although Governor Jennings remained in occupation, and on 25 April 1736 Prince Frederick (father of George III), welcomed his bride Augusta of Saxe-Gotha there on her arrival in England: his own grandfather, George I (d. 1737), had also spent the night there on his landing at Greenwich from Hanover in 1714, as successor to Queen Anne. From 1743 the Governor lived in the Hospital and the formidable Lady Katharine Pelham, wife of Prime Minister Henry Pelham, became Park Ranger. In 1745 £3,000 was spent on it for her, with another £1,700 by 1747, but no further details are known, nor is it clear how the Pelhams used it; presumably only occasionally, though it was referred to at the time as both 'Pelham House' and the 'Ranger's House'. Henry died in 1754 and Lady Katharine's 37-year personal tenancy, to her death in 1780, was the longest in its history.

William III (1650–1702) and Mary II (1662–94), in the ceiling of the Painted Hall, Greenwich, by Sir James Thornhill, 1708–12

William and Mary were Stuarts. Mary was the elder daughter of James, Duke of York, by his first wife, Anne Hyde (d. 1671), daughter of the Earl of Clarendon. William, as Willem III, Prince of Orange, was son of Willem II and Mary, eldest daughter of Charles I and Henrietta Maria. Both were Protestants, and Willem – like his father – was leader of the United Provinces of the Netherlands against persistent Catholic threats. In 1688 he accepted the English invitation to depose his Catholic-convert father-in-law, James II, as much to secure the Dutch position against Louis XIV of France as for any other reason. Since Mary had the direct claim to the throne, she is here shown slightly higher and they were crowned as 'joint monarchs' in 1689. He took precedence when in England but she ruled in her own right when, as often, he was in the Netherlands. She was the prime founder of Greenwich Hospital for seamen but rejected Wren's original design since it blocked the view which, by that time, 'her' Queen's House had gained towards the Thames. Neither Mary nor William used Greenwich; on his death, Mary's younger sister Anne succeeded him as the last Stuart monarch (1702–14).

The Greenwich Foundation for the Old Royal Naval College

London and the River Thames from One Tree Hill, Greenwich Park,
by Jan Griffier the Elder, c.*1690*

This painting from the 1690s makes up in incident and detail for its deficiencies in perspective. It effectively conveys the privileged nature of access to the Park at the time and also the busy shipping of the Thames. This made Greenwich a world-renowned landmark as international maritime trade passed to and from London, itself already one of Europe's greatest ports.

Naval vessels are also present and the churches too were landmarks: old St Alfege's at Greenwich – before its roof collapsed in a storm in 1710 – and St Nicholas's at Deptford, close to its Royal Dockyard. London can be seen beyond the mills of Millwall on the opposite side of the river. The painting adds little about the Queen's House or Palace site, the latter very much in transition.

What it does provide is another variation on the formal garden layout north of the House, to compare with the 1693 survey plan (p. 45). As in that, the stump of the tiltyard tower still stands but here surrounded by a rectilinear layout of gravel walks and lawns, each with a single cypress tree at its centre.
BHC1833

The barge built for use on the Thames by Frederick, Prince of Wales (1707–51), eldest son of George II (who outlived him, George III being Frederick's son). Its designer, William Kent, was the leading architect of the 18th-century Palladian revival in England, under the patronage of the Earl of Burlington. The native hero of the movement was, of course, Inigo Jones, whose *Designs* Kent also edited and published for Burlington in 1727. Of these, Burlington then had a very important collection, especially Jones's designs for Stuart court masques. These later passed by inheritance into the Devonshire collection at Chatsworth. When Princess Augusta of Saxe-Gotha landed at Greenwich to marry Prince Frederick on 25 April 1736, she stayed two nights in the Queen's House, before her formal entry to London. The Prince came down (by land) to dine with her in the House on the 26th, but news reports show he went back that evening 'in his barge'. After his death it became the principal royal barge until last used by Prince Albert for the opening of the London Coal Exchange in 1849 (see below, from the *Illustrated London News*). It is still Crown property, originally put on loan to the Museum by George VI.

D9523-3, BAE0035 (Lent by Her Majesty The Queen)

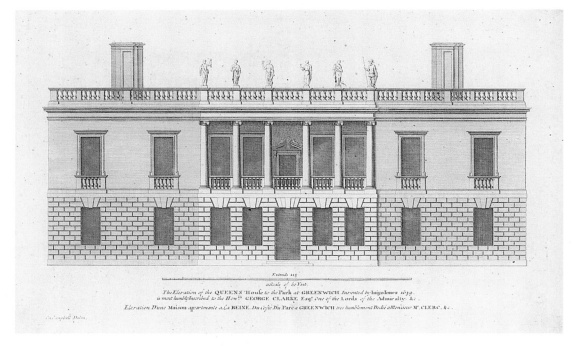

Extends 115
a Scale of 80 Feet.
The Elevation of the QUEENS House to the Park at GREENWICH Invented by Inigo Iones 1639.
is most humbly Inscribed to the Hon.ble GEORGE CLARKE Esq.r One of the Lords of the Admiralty &c.
Elevation D'une Maison appertenante a La REINE. Du Cofté Du Parc a GREENWICH tres humblement Dedié aMonsieur M.r CLERC, &c.

C. Campbell Delin.

Although there is an early north-front elevation drawing (see p. 31), the earliest of the south side as built is by John James, about 1710–20. This print is the one published in 1715 by Colen Campbell (later briefly the Surveyor to Greenwich Hospital) in the first volume of his *Vitruvius Britannicus* – an important compilation on British buildings and the founding manual of 18th-century Palladianism.

While convincing, it is slightly misleading. The statues shown may echo a preliminary sketch by Jones (see p. 30) but were never added. More subtly, Campbell suggests the 1708 lengthening of the lower windows, but the original proportions of all appear slightly further idealised. In the balustrading of the loggia he also accurately follows Palladio, in putting a space rather than an upright at centre, where James

suggests that Jones, at least in this case, did not. The 1930s loggia restoration follows James, with the result today that it is normally closed to the public since the spaces are now considered a health-and-safety risk to small children, which the textbook Palladian arrangement could resolve.

PAH3292

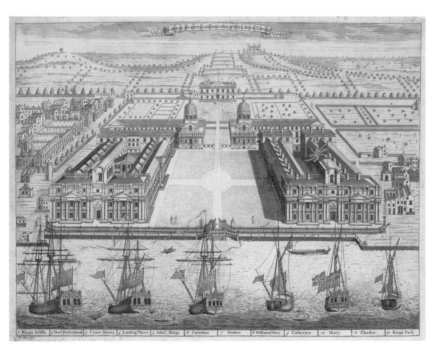

One of many similar 'prospect' prints of Greenwich Hospital with the Queen's House beyond. Their effect – well before this was reinforced by 19th-century changes on site – is to promote the misconception that the House's north façade has always been the front (as it appears today). Most are substantially imaginary but this one shows the 'Giant Steps' up to the Observatory, and the line of Romney Road which did not continue east (left), as Trafalgar Road, until 1825–28. Little is known of the House's formal 18th-century north gardens, only hinted at here, but they included a fountain. Fed from a cistern in the building, it stood in the middle of today's west lawn. The Queen Anne Court (lower left) was incomplete when the print was issued but it does include the temporary Hospital chapel built between its two wings in 1707. The domed Queen Mary Court behind, which holds the permanent one, was not started until 1735. The arched turret on the roof of the King Charles Court (lower right) was added in 1718 and removed in 1733; that on the Queen Anne Court was never built. The 'yatchs' make the point that Greenwich was the London hub for royal and diplomatic comings and goings to the Continent. PAJ4031

Greenwich Hospital from the North Bank of the Thames, by Canaletto, c.1752

The Venetian painter Giovanni Antonio Canal, known as Canaletto, worked in England from 1746 to 1755 and his famous picture shows the Hospital as completed in 1751. Artistic inaccuracies aside, details show he knew the view first-hand. Dr Samuel Johnson called the Hospital 'too magnificent for a place of charity', but its splendour deliberately proclaimed to passing ships, the nation and the wider world that the British Crown would care for seamen injured in its naval service, in an age which only knew charitable forms of public welfare. The picture also shows the key role of the Queen's House in the 'Grand Axis' architectural composition. Wren originally intended a three-sided Hospital open to the Thames, with a large-domed chapel in front of the House, until Queen Mary II specified retention of its open view to the river. Wren's ingenious solution was four courts flanking this 'visto', with twin domes on the inner ones, over the Chapel (left) and Painted Hall (right). On flat ground, the House would look under-scale; but with the rising Park ascent to Wren's offset, quirky, red-brick Observatory behind, it is an effective terminus. The pitch of the roof over the Hall is exaggerated, but was formerly more noticeable than today.

BHC1827 (Caird Collection)

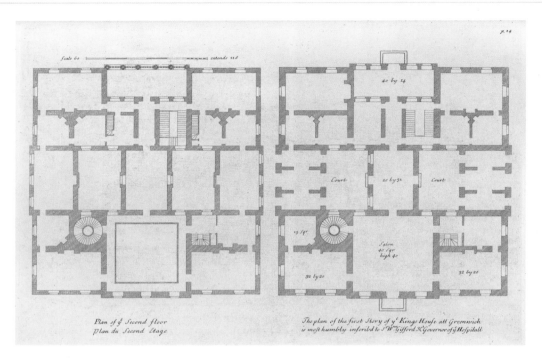

Plan of ỹ Second floor
Plan du Second Etage

The plan of the first Story of ỹ Kings House att Greenwich
is most humbly inscribd to Sʳ Wᵐ Gifford K Governor of ỹ Hospitall

Plans of (left) the top floor of the House and (right) the ground floor, from *Vitruvius Britannicus*. The south or Park side is at the top and the 1662 East and West Bridge Rooms are shown supported on their original pillared arches, with side passages, of which only the outer pillars now (largely) remain as part of the flanking walls. The top floor includes two small sets of stairs, flanking the South Stairs.

These go up to servants' attics installed in 1661–62 over lowered ceilings in the rooms concerned; they were reconstructed in the 1980s restoration. The room measurements shown are nominal rather than precise but make the point that Jones was generally using dimensions divisible by 5 and 4, i.e. 15, 20, 32, 40. The 40-foot-cube Hall has a hidden equivalent on the south side, of which loggia and Orangery are

the outer part. The layout of other features may have been aided by geometry. The obvious example is the north terrace (not shown), whose depth was determined by a circle of which the centre is the intersection of the plan diagonals under the Centre Bridge, and the radius the distance to the House's corners. L4552

Admiral Sir John Jennings (1664–1743), by Sir Godfrey Kneller, 1708–09

Jennings was regarded as the finest seaman of his time, but had few chances for glory as an admiral. As a captain in the War of the Spanish Succession he served under Admiral Rooke at the Battle of Vigo (1702), at the British capture of Gibraltar and the Battle of Malaga (both 1704), and was knighted by Queen Anne later that year. He was eventually commander-in-chief in the Mediterranean and a Lord of the Admiralty to 1727, when deafness prompted him to retire. In 1720 he became Governor of Greenwich Hospital and Ranger of the Park, and – as the longest-serving Governor – enjoyed 23 years' use of the Queen's House as his official residence, to his death. Jennings's visible legacy at Greenwich is the – now eroded – statue of George II by John Michael Rysbrack in the Grand Square of the Hospital (Old Royal Naval College). Rooke captured the large marble block in the Mediterranean, about 1704. The Hospital bought it but it lay unused until Jennings personally paid Rysbrack £400 to carve the statue, installed in 1735. This portrait is one of a set of the leading naval officers of Anne's reign, painted for her and her husband Prince George, by Kneller and Michael Dahl.

BHC2805 (Greenwich Hospital Collection)

Henry Pelham (1694–1754), Prime Minister and First Lord of the Treasury, after William Hoare, 1752

Pelham was the son of the 1st Baron Pelham; Thomas, his elder half-brother, became the first Duke of Newcastle in 1715, and both were notable Whig statesmen. Henry was appointed Lord of the Treasury in 1721 under Robert Walpole, who had justifiably high regard for his abilities and relied greatly on both his and Newcastle's support. In 1742 he succeeded Walpole as Prime Minister, with Newcastle in his cabinet. He was tactful, peace-loving and held to be weak, but a master of Parliamentary and financial business. In 1746, when George II proved uncooperative, both brothers resigned but (as they intended) obliged him to reappoint them two days later because no-one else could form a ministry. Pelham had his wife Katharine appointed Ranger of Greenwich Park in 1743. After considerable expenditure on the Queen's House, they probably used it from 1745 as a private retreat but no precise details are known. He died in 1754, when Newcastle became Prime Minister in his place. Pelham's lasting legacy is the British change from the 'Old Style' Julian to the 'New Style' Gregorian calendar in 1752, the dates 3–13 September being omitted from that year in Britain, to fall in line with the rest of Europe.

PAG6357

The Right Honble Henry Pelham
Chancellor, and Under Treasurer of the
Honble Privy Council, and One of

First Lord Commissioner of y.^e Treasury
Exchequer, one of His Majesty's Most
the Lords of the Regency.

'The Ton at Greenwich. A la Festoon dans le Park à Greenwich', 1777

This print may refer to Lady Katharine Pelham (1700/01–80), Ranger of Greenwich Park and chatelaine of the Queen's House from 1743 to her death, though there is no comparative image of her to confirm it. This is surprising since she was daughter of the Duke of Rutland, devoted wife of a Prime Minister and, even after his death in 1754, an influential manipulator of patronage in her family's interests. Pelham's successor and her brother-in-law, the Duke of Newcastle, was himself an impressive figure but stood in awe of her. In 1761 he was caught in an unenviable quandary over nominating an MP and, as Sir Lewis Namier put it, 'between the upper and nether millstone, the King [George III] and Lady Katharine Pelham…hardly knew which was the more formidable'. He managed to pacify both, and his resignation in 1762 clipped Lady Pelham's public but not her private wings. How and how often she used the House is unknown, but since she also had a fine London home, it was likely more often in summer. This print is a satire on French-influenced fashions prevalent just before her death and on the introduction from Europe of umbrellas (here carried by a servant), an innovation also scorned by Dr Johnson.

PAH3334

THE TON AT GREENWICH.
A LÁ FESTOON DANS LE PARK A GREENWICH

An engraving showing the House at the end of Lady Pelham's tenure as Ranger of the Park. By this time the Park had limited public access, for Pensioners of Greenwich Hospital and other respectable people. The walls shown were probably improved in the 18th century, but by the mid-1690s there was already an elm tree nursery to the east of the House and a garden to the west, both enclosed by walls dropping back to its corners. These must also have been high to keep out the deer (only confined to the 'Wilderness' in the south-east corner of the Park in 1927). The House's view to the Park was never blocked but the railings (perhaps gated) were probably inserted after it was allocated as a residence for the Governor of Greenwich Hospital in 1708, who also doubled as Ranger until 1743. The roadway arches are walled in, have rooms under them, and have lost the Bridge Room balconies above. The building on the right, on the old road, is a detached kitchen added by John James in 1723 for Governor Jennings in an area that already had other service buildings. The walls shown were only 25 feet (7.6 metres) south of the House, much closer than today.

PAJ2659

Greenwich Park, by 'I.M.', March 1749

A print from the *London Magazine* with a view of the Queen's House (south front) under its title of the 'Ranger's House', early in Lady Pelham's tenancy as Park Ranger. The Observatory and the hill on which it stands are identified respectively as 'Flamstead House' and 'Flamstead Hill'. The vanished Keeper's House can be seen (near the modern bandstand). André Le Nôtre's 1660s layout of tree avenues and 'rounds' is clearly shown, including the 'great cross avenue' running through the Park, east to west at the base of the hill. Along with the 'rounds', this cross avenue has now largely vanished. 'Sir James Creed's' ground (Creed Place) is identified at the extreme left end of 'Park Wall' (Park Vista) lower left, below the first 'Burying Ground' of Greenwich Hospital. This was in use from 1707 to 1749 but was largely built over in the 19th century.

PAD2184

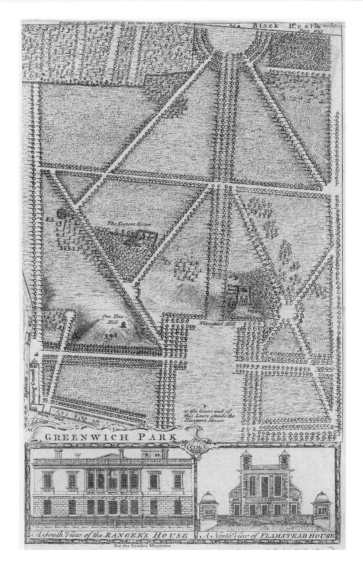

The Queen's House from the north-east, by John Charnock, late 18th century

After today's Romney Road was established in 1697–99, walls went up on both sides, with gates on the axis of the House. This was necessary for the security of the Greenwich Hospital site and the privacy of the House in the Ranger's/Governor's use. Today's railings only replaced these walls around 1860, and until then views to north or south from the public road were restricted. This is at present the only known one of the north side of the House. It was drawn, probably about 1790, among a huge number of often much odder building studies by Charnock. He lived locally and is better known as a naval biographer. Given the neglected ground that fronts the terrace, it may illustrate the period when those in charge were accused of making 'a hogstye of the house and a cow house of the premises'. Steps have been added on the east (and west) side of the terrace, flanking the retaining walls to a kitchen building and yard on the east side and a garden on the west. The distant wall, with St Alfege's Church behind, conceals another garden strip (see p. 93), and the eastern side of the 1749–1857 Hospital burial ground.

PAF3012

'The West India Docks…with Greenwich Hospital in the foreground. Drawn in the Camera Obscura…', 1804

While the new docks appear in the distance, this is more important as a record of the House in its immediate setting in 1804, traced (a little oddly) from the image projected by the camera obscura then in the east pavilion of Flamsteed House at the Observatory, and still there today in reconstructed form. It shows the 1720s detached kitchen on the east side and an enclosed garden on the west, both with retaining walls separating them from the lower-level 'field' to the north, itself walled off from Romney Road in front of the Hospital. The walled ground beyond the small building on the left remained the 'Governor's Garden' until what is now the NMM's West Wing was built on it in 1862. The western (left) roadway arch of the House is also walled up, with windows into the room under it. Most intriguingly, a carriage is drawn up below the loggia. This suggests that the railings (not shown but see p. 90) into the Park in front were gated and that the Orangery was perhaps still a formal entrance at this time. If so, it would likely have been in the preceding century, when the House was the Ranger's official residence.

PAD2204

SCHOOL DAYS
1806–1933

The caretakers in neglectful charge by 1792 were reputedly using the House as the centre of a smuggling ring, but in 1795 it was fit for Caroline of Brunswick's reception in England for her (disastrous) marriage to George, Prince of Wales, later George IV. In 1805, separated from him and living at Montagu House, Blackheath, she was nonetheless appointed Ranger of the Park. She remained at Montagu House, however, and that became the Ranger's House. This change resulted from a costing exercise and a proposal that the Queen's House become the new home of the Royal Naval Asylum, whose President from 1805 was George's brother Ernest, Duke of Cumberland. The Asylum, an orphanage school for the children (boys and girls) of naval seamen, had been established in Paddington in the 1790s. After early difficulties, it was granted £20,000 by Parliament in 1805, partly to find a larger home; and Caroline, as Ranger, was paid £7,875 to cede the Queen's House in October 1806. Asylum staff and the first 70 girls took up residence there in November 1807, after the start of a century of drastic alterations which eventually left only the Hall, the 1660s King's Presence Chamber and the East Bridge Room relatively undamaged. In 1809 Daniel Alexander's flanking colonnades with terminating wings were completed, but the latter – originally short – were extended north by 1811. From 1821, the Asylum was combined, under Greenwich Hospital, with the Hospital school for the sons of seamen (founded 1712–15). The Asylum intake became the junior or 'Lower School', and until 1841 the House – or 'Centre Building' as it became known – provided quarters for up to 200 girls, who had a segregated walled garden area to the north. They trained for domestic service and the boys – occupying the wings – for careers at sea, after 1848 solely in the Navy or, later, as Royal Marines. In 1841 – which also saw pupil disturbances that prompted rapid educational reforms – girls' schooling ended and the House was further altered to become mainly staff apartments, with the West Bridge Room as a staff library. The central roadway had been fully enclosed under Lady Pelham, and the School had two roof-lit ground-level rooms in the open wells between the top-floor bridges: by 1875 that to the east was a School 'Museum' – though what it held is not yet known. A staff garden on the south side was separated from the Park by a low wall and ditch to keep its deer out, and railings between the south-side colonnading kept children out. The colonnades gave sheltered play space, which eventually looked over a huge asphalt parade ground to the north. From 1843, in front of the House and originally in the walled girls' enclosure until it was demolished, stood the first of three full-size, full-rigged 'model ships', the last (1873) called *Fame*: on these the boys learnt the arts of seamanship under sail. Vocational, technical and regimented, by the 1850s the School was highly regarded and its output ably self-reliant. The elite navigational students of the Upper School were routinely placed in training posts in HM ships, many becoming commissioned officers, including a few admirals. In 1892 Queen Victoria recognised its achievements: hitherto the 'Greenwich Hospital Schools', it became instead the 'Royal Hospital School'.

Princess Caroline arriving at Greenwich in the Royal Yacht Princess Augusta, *5 April 1795,* *after Nicholas Pocock, 1800*

A print from the *Naval Chronicle* of March 1800. It shows the *Princess Augusta* surrounded by other shipping and small boats as she heads up Blackwall reach towards Greenwich Hospital, here seen from the north-east. The yacht flies the Royal Standard and the broad pendant of Commodore John Willett Payne. All the vessels are heading up on a fresh breeze to land Princess Caroline of Brunswick at Greenwich, where she was welcomed in the Queen's House, prior to her marriage to George, Prince of Wales (later George IV). On disembarking to a reception including massed ranks of Greenwich Pensioners, she was overheard to remark (in French), 'Are all Englishmen missing an arm or a leg?' Greenwich was the usual point of departure and arrival for royal comings and goings between London and Europe in the sailing yachts. Often more than one was used (or other small naval vessels) for family members, retainers and baggage. Armed naval escort was added outside the Thames.

PAD2198

'View of the Naval Asylum at Greenwich', c.1810

This small print is the only image yet found which clearly shows the original short length of the terminating wings to the Queen's House colonnades, added in 1807–09. These are by Daniel Asher Alexander (1768–1846), who designed many institutional buildings – including, at this time, the famous prison on Dartmoor (originally for French prisoners of war). He was present at the Asylum directors' discussion about expanding accommodation and was given the job after slipping a note to its President, HRH the Duke of Cumberland, saying any additions to the House should be 'in strict accordance with the style of Inigo Jones'. His initial wings (the west one seen here) were rapidly outgrown and were extended north by 1811. They had boys' dormitories on the upper floors with schoolrooms and other facilities below and, when lengthened, included a chapel in the west wing and an enlarged dining room in the east. Further extensions were added from 1862 on the west side. The print also shows the new, low Park wall with an excavated ditch on the south side. This replaced the high 18th-century wall (see p. 90) and opened up the view to the Park while continuing to exclude deer. It is 50 feet (15 metres) further into the Park, on extra ground granted in 1808. The central door shown is also still there.

PAI8815

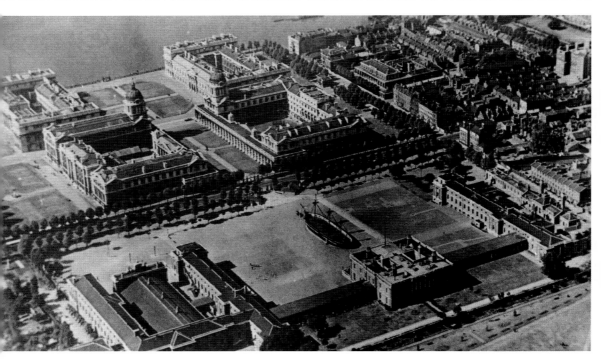

An aerial view probably taken about 1925, with the Queen's House and most of the 19th-century additions made to what, from 1892, became the Royal Hospital School in the foreground. To the lower left, the 1873 gymnasium ('Neptune's Hall') has been added in the courtyard formed by the L-shaped west- and south-wing additions of 1862. In the parade ground north of the House, only the lower masts of the training ship *Fame* remain standing (see p. 106). Beyond the east wing (right), what is now the NMM car park holds School service buildings, including the bakery, tailoring workshop and laundry; here the boys did most of the work as part of 'trades' training, in what was a near self-sufficient enclosed community. At the extreme lower right are two of the three domes of the small School observatory, begun in the 1850s under the headmastership of the Revd George Fisher (see p. 102). The 18th- and 19th-century houses on Park Row immediately above and below its intersection with Romney Road (upper right) were lost to World War II bombing.

P47503

School adaptations

In its School days, the House was usually called the 'Centre Building' and this plan (based on a published one of the whole site) shows its ground floor in 1875. It was by then largely divided into four senior staff houses including the Headmaster's and naval Captain-Superintendent's: each had bedrooms above and kitchens in the basements (the southern ones being dug-out for the School). The 18th-century room under the Centre Bridge had been reduced to a north-south corridor, and larger ground-floor ones on either side had oval skylights into the east and west light wells above. Though previously used as classrooms (see p. 104), these now held a reading room for the naval (technical) teaching staff, and the School Museum. This was proposed by the Revd Fisher (see p. 102) 'for the use and improvement of the boys' early in 1851, when estimates and 'a list of articles contributed' for it were drawn up. In August 1853, when decoration was being finished, the British Museum frostily declined an Admiralty request for 'any objects of interest they can spare' for it. The contents of the Museum are not yet clear, though the School still holds items probably displayed there. The dotted lines across the roadway indicate the bridge vaults. The small areas outside windows are basement light wells, still there on the Park side (top).

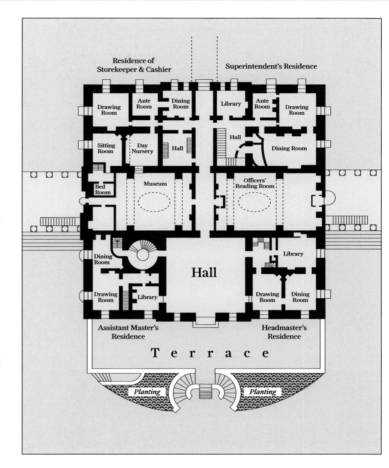

Naval School, Greenwich & Block Model Ship

The first drill ship, modelled on a naval brig and constructed in front of the Queen's House in 1843, for the 'sea exercises' of boys of the Greenwich Hospital School. It was built for £250 using old timber from the Hospital and redundant ship parts from Chatham Dockyard. The work was done largely by the School carpenters and the boys, directed by the one-legged and energetic John Wood Rouse, the School's Lieutenant-Superintendent of Industrial Training. Boys are shown 'manning the yards', as they did for visiting dignitaries (see also p. 95, from a music-cover *c.*1850). The surrounding walled garden area had been a segregated play space for the girls resident in the House until the School became 'boys only' in 1841. This ship and the walls were demolished in 1860–61 and a second vessel constructed. In 1872–73 this was replaced by a third, called *Fame*, whose hull lasted until the School left Greenwich in 1933. It was then cleared away when the site was converted for use as the National Maritime Museum. The first two seem to have been unnamed, although 'Princess Royal' was reportedly suggested for the one shown here. The three vessels dominated the northern view of the House for 90 years, especially after railings replaced the walls along Romney Road in the early 1860s.

PAD2249, PA18017 (p. 95)

The School's gates and Fame, *c.1906*

By the time this local postcard (top) was made, the 1860s School railings and fine late-19th-century gates were in position, with two small porters' lodges just inside. The training 'block' ship shown is the third, called *Fame* (see pp. 106–07). The Turkish bronze gun (1790/1) under the bow was taken by Admiral Sir John Duckworth from Kinaliada Island, off modern Istanbul in the Sea of Marmara, in a brief Turkish campaign of 1807 and was presented to the Royal Naval Asylum by the Duke of Cumberland in 1818, with an added inscription recording the Asylum's origins. It was taken to the new School in 1933, but in 2007 returned to stand outside the World Heritage Site visitor information centre at the Old Royal Naval College. The oval photograph (right) taken about 1850 shows it still inside the walled garden area in front of the Queen's House (see opposite page).

A1727, H0804

The Revd George Fisher (1794–1873), Headmaster and Principal of the Greenwich Hospital Schools, c.1860

Fisher's father, a surveyor, died when Fisher was about four. At the age of 14 he joined an insurance company to help support his mother but attracted attention for his scientific interests. He entered St Catherine's College, Cambridge, in 1816, but only graduated in 1821 and became MA in 1825. This was both due to illness and because, in 1818, he went as astronomer on an Arctic expedition beyond Spitsbergen in search of a passage to the Bering Strait. In 1821–23, now a naval chaplain (to 1832), he sailed as astronomer on Parry's North-West Passage expedition and was elected a member of the Royal Society in 1825. In 1834 he was appointed Headmaster and Chaplain of the Greenwich Hospital Schools, which then (and to 1945) had a Captain-Superintendent with supporting instructor officers in disciplinary control, and a separate academic teaching staff. The School saw difficulties in his early years but Fisher took good advice, wrote textbooks on algebra and geometry to introduce modern methods, and built a School observatory to assist scientific and navigational training. By 1851 an inspector reported the Upper School 'far beyond any other known to me in scientific attainment'. In 1860 Fisher became Principal, retiring in 1863.

H4583

*John Riddle (1816–62) with his class of navigational pupils
at the School*, c.1855

John Riddle was the son and successor of Edward Riddle (c.1786–1854) who was the mathematical master of the Upper School of Greenwich Hospital from 1821, the year it absorbed the Royal Naval Asylum, until his retirement in 1851. Edward was a significant teacher whose most important work was a *Treatise on Navigation and Nautical Astronomy* (1824), 'which provided a complete course of mathematics for sailors, combining theory and practice in a way which had not been attempted before'. It became a standard work and saw eight editions to 1864. His son John, an equally good teacher, followed him as Headmaster of the Upper School and was also examiner in navigation to the government Department of Science and Art. His end was sadly accidental: on 25 September 1862, he stood on a stool in class to reach a book down, slipped and fell, banging his head. 'On rising quickly, he playfully remarked "That's an awkward blow, boys"' but quickly lost consciousness and died on 11 October, aged 46, leaving a widow and six young children.

H1347

This is one of a group of very early School photographs. It shows one of the rooms then in the central roadway of the Queen's House in use as a schoolroom, and appears to have been taken from between the Centre Bridge and the inner arch of either the East or West Bridge Room. The door in the back wall, under the outer arch, leads to the colonnade beyond. These were only ground-floor rooms, and light is coming from a skylight in the roof set between the Bridges at that level, with open light wells above. By this time the large 18th-century room installed under the Centre Bridge in the early 18th century had been removed and replaced by a narrower passage. This connected the Hall to the south-side central corridor of the House across the roadway, with access doors into the rooms on either side. In 1908 the Hall, passage, south corridor, and the walls of the Orangery on the south side were given a unifying mock-historic cladding of dark plywood panelling to just under doorway height. This was removed in the 1930s restoration.

H1328

'Divisions' at a Royal prize-giving, 10 July 1890

The Hospital School has always had a marching band, and School parades and inspections by divisions still take place regularly at Holbrook, Suffolk, its home since 1933. This wood engraving from the *Illustrated London News* shows 'divisions' on the annual prize-giving day in 1890, with the salute being taken by HRH The Prince of Wales, later King Edward VII. As noted in the report: 'At the conclusion of … luncheon, the Royal party adjourned to the terrace [of the Queen's House] to witness the musical drill and other evolutions performed by the scholars, who number 1,100.' Here the School marches past the 'horseshoe stairs' of the House where the Royal Standard flies and the Prince raises his hat in salute. The detail at top right shows prizes being handed out in Neptune's Hall, the large gymnasium of 1873 (now replaced by Neptune Court), which had a stage at the south end, though according to news reports this was done by the Princess (left) rather than the Prince on this occasion.

H1458

'Training Ship, Royal Hospital School, Greenwich', c.1900

Fame was the third and largest of the School's three training ships; she was also the best built, by Green's of Blackwall, the last great builders of Indiamen (see p. 74). Though barely finished, she was formally named by the daughter of Admiral Sir Alexander Milne on 21 July 1873, the day before he did the honours at the School's annual prize-giving in the Great Hall of the Queen's House. The upper masts were removed about 1914 for safety, after sail training ended, and the hull was demolished in 1934–35.

The whole beakhead, bearing the figurehead of Fame with a trumpet, had then already gone to the new school at Holbrook and still looks out dramatically over the playing fields there from the end of its small-bore rifle range (below); the stern decoration, showing the arms of Greenwich Hospital, was bought for the Mariners Museum, Newport News, Virginia, and can still be seen there. This local postcard view (left) dates to around 1900.
H1277

'Cricket on the Asphalte', 1898

One of the illustrations from an article on the School in the *Navy and Army Illustrated* of 10 September 1898. What are now the main Museum lawns were by then an asphalt parade ground, used for that purpose and as a playground, as shown here. This image just shows the stern of *Fame* (left) and the still-visible slope of the ground flanking the Queen's House, from the front line of the terrace up to the base of the colonnade steps. This may originally have been more marked and is why the north side of the House was on raised foundations. In the 1934–36 Museum conversion, the former parade ground was levelled and the slope transformed into a steeper, grassed bank up to the colonnades, with four sets of stone steps in the building angles. The apparently grimy state of the House is a little deceptive, since at this time the buildings were all painted mushroom brown, against which the stonework here appears clean. Greenwich did suffer from high levels of atmospheric pollution, however. In 1905, partly for that reason, Admiral Sir John Fisher called Greenwich a 'most unsuitable' place for naval education and 'the surroundings of the [Naval] College... practically one huge slum.'

H1393

MODERN TIMES
1934—TODAY

In the 1920s, plans to transfer the School to Holbrook, Suffolk – where it moved in 1933 – coincided with those to found the National Maritime Museum, established by Act of Parliament in 1934. In 1927 it was announced that the Museum would take over the old School buildings at Greenwich, and in late 1934 HM Office of Works began a massive restoration of the Queen's House, led by George Chettle, architect and Inspector of Ancient Monuments. The most striking external change was demolition of the rooms blocking the central roadway since before 1708, which also opened the full east–west vista along the colonnades for the first time. The interior was returned as closely as possible to its earliest form, retention of the 1660s Bridge Rooms and the outer sash windows being among inevitable compromises. As publicly opened in 1937, the House was spartan: plain off-white walls displayed portraits and marine paintings (with some glass-cased ship models), telling the early story of Britain's rise to seaborne Empire under the Tudors and Stuarts, and of 'Old Greenwich'. Treasures were removed during World War II, and the House was largely closed, save for a morale-boosting display in the Hall and some requisitioned naval use. Blast damage from near-misses was slight and an incendiary-bomb fire on the top floor quickly put out. After essential repairs, the House reopened in April 1947, though further renovation continued for some time.

By 1975 there had been little essential change beyond an increase in glass-cased exhibits and roughly 'period' furnishing of some upper rooms to suggest the House's original uses. The conflict was – and is – between museum use and respecting the House's architectural significance and early role. This was reattempted in the second major restoration of 1984–89, which put back 'Jonesian' design elements in replica form, including fire surrounds and authentic early windows onto the roadway. The top floor was readjusted to 1660s layout, with replacement of original features taken out in the 1930s. The Queen's Side was lavishly refitted with well-researched replica furniture, silk wall hangings and fibre-optic light fittings. The paintings originally in the Hall ceiling were reinstalled as 'computer-painted' copies and a period paint scheme was also recreated. As before, the historic paintings displayed were no later than about 1710 and, on the top floor, there were no glass cases. In 1998–99 both a lift and new staircase, from basement up, also replaced a service stair off the Hall's south-west corner.

From 1990 the 'furnished House' much expanded its audience, notably welcoming families and children, despite some critical disdain among specialists. It also began a new career as a successful event and wedding venue, but in 1999 it was emptied to hold the Museum's millennial *Story of Time* exhibition.

Since then, presentation has been sympathetic but not 'historic', and the rooms have showcased aspects of the Museum's superb paintings collection and occasional art exhibitions. In October 2016, after over a year of refurbishment, the House reopened with new displays of fine and decorative art, including significant loans, to mark the 400th anniversary of its commissioning and design. Its next century will no doubt see similar programmes to preserve its significance and re-present it in new ways to following generations.

The School left Greenwich in March 1933 but the Museum did not formally take over the site until 1934. This was in the depths of the Depression, which saw local efforts to provide some holiday relief, including the building of 'Greenwich Beach' by spreading thousands of tons of seaside sand on the Thames foreshore of the Royal Naval College. For a week from 23 September 1933 this funfair was also set up in front of the House round the dismasted hulk of the *Fame* in aid of two local hospitals. It proved controversial. Under the headline 'Greenwich Fair "Storm"', the *Kentish Mercury* of 22 September reported that it was only taking place after a last-minute conference between the Admiralty and other interested parties, and a liquor licence was specifically refused. A later issue noted the incongruity between the 'garish caravans and drab motor lorries' and the 'venerable old edifice', and both printed strongly worded letters of complaint at this use of the grounds. The Admiral President of the Royal Naval College also pointed out that valuable items destined for the new Museum were already being stored in the Queen's House. The event was a popular success, however. The tower in the distance on the right is that of St Mary's Church, designed by George Basevi in 1823. This was demolished in 1935–36, and from 2011 its site became the approach to the Museum's new Sammy Ofer Wing entrance.

D9469-9

The most noticeable change here was reconstruction of the Portland stone balustrade of the loggia (see p. 71) according to the early-18th-century record drawing made by John James. Here the columns are shown linked by the previous iron safety railing whose exact date of installation is not known. The original railings between the Tuscan columns of the south-side colonnades can also just be seen. These excluded the children of the Royal Naval Asylum and, from 1821, the combined Greenwich Hospital Schools from general access to the south-side staff garden area. However, there are images of senior boys being instructed in the use of navigational and other instruments there. In the foreground is the 'ha-ha' wall and dry ditch – though in a true ha-ha, no wall is visible from the house side. This was built around 1809 after the Asylum moved in. Most of the bricks seem to have been recycled from the 18th-century wall (see p. 90) which was closer to the House. The ditch was partly backfilled and first planted as a Park border in 1925.

D9469-007

QUEEN'S HOUSE - FIRST FLOOR. 4.

In these two contrasting images, the doorway leads into the south-east corner room on the top floor, which after insertion of the East Bridge Room (behind the camera here) became the King's Bedchamber. Another door to the right links to a private 'writing closet' with access via an outer closet to the South Stairs. The fire surround is the one installed in the 1630s. In the 1980s restoration the panelling was oak-grained and this is how the room appears on the left, in 1990. Above the fire hangs Willem van de Velde the Younger's 1658 painting of a calm with a Dutch flagship and States yacht coming to anchor, formerly in the collection of Sir Bruce Ingram, owner and editor of the *Illustrated London News* (which his grandfather founded) and one of the key early supporters of the Museum from the 1920s until his death in 1963. The restored King's Bedchamber lies beyond the open door, with the rush-matting floor covering initially used in the furnished presentation.

D4940, H1140

An image which clearly shows how the spaces under all three Bridges had been filled in from the early 18th century on; also how, in the early or mid-1700s, the pillared inner arches of the 1660s Bridge Rooms above were converted to the same single vault as Jones's Centre Bridge to make the insertion of rooms under them practical. As is shown here, Jones's arch comprises two side vaults with a gap between. Though now infilled it is here empty, giving a tall space between the large doors that, probably from the building of Lord Romney's 'middle salon' around 1700, allowed the Hall and south corridor to be linked – as also shown – at the same floor level. During the School era, if not before, large ground-floor rooms illuminated by skylights were built in the open wells between the three Bridges. They were apparently originally schoolrooms but by 1875 the eastern one was the School Museum, the western the 'Officers' Reading Room'. The East and West Colonnades were thus entirely separated and their paving level was also higher than that of the original roadway. When this was restored to its 17th-century level, short steps on either side of the House had to be added to provide through access under it once more.

D9469-012

Early moves to house a 'national naval and nautical museum' at Greenwich centred on the Queen's House alone. Although the House was recognised as too small, Greenwich Hospital (a charitable directorate within the Admiralty since 1884) was initially reluctant to include the other School buildings. The Government nonetheless did so under the National Maritime Museum Act of 1934, with reversion to the Hospital should the Museum ever leave. George VI was welcomed to open the Museum in front of the House on 27 April 1937. Here Lord Stanhope, the Chairman of Trustees, presents a golden key to Queen Elizabeth to unlock the terrace door to the Hall, with the King (in naval uniform) and Princess Elizabeth looking on. The Museum's founding Director, Professor Geoffrey Callender, stands on the right, in profile against the door. Callender became Sir Geoffrey in 1938 and the Museum was created almost entirely according to his personal conception of it. The same applied to its immediately post-World War II reconstruction since, owing to wartime disruptions, he was still in command when he died suddenly in his office of a heart attack on 6 November 1946, three weeks before his 71st birthday.

D9455-4

A photograph taken after the King's speech at the opening of the Museum in the old Neptune Hall on 27 April 1937. Front row, left to right: Sir Samuel Hoare, First Lord of the Admiralty; Princess Elizabeth (the present Queen) standing in front of Admiral Sir George Hope, President of the Society for Nautical Research; HM King George VI and Queen Elizabeth; HM Queen Mary, the King's mother; Sir James Caird (1864–1954), the Museum's principal founding benefactor. This was the first such event

Princess Elizabeth attended, the week after her 11th birthday and nearly three weeks before her parents' coronation on 12 May. The model representing Charles I's *Sovereign of the Seas*, the first 100-gun vessel in the Navy, was first exhibited at the Great Exhibition of 1851. At least two of the carvers who worked on the elaborate decoration of the ship itself, launched at Woolwich in 1637, also did carved work in the Queen's House (see p. 54).

D9469-056

Many of the Museum's few early staff members were called up during World War II. The Director, Sir Geoffrey Callender, spent most of it in remote control from Oxford, with his Establishment Officer, the competent 'Reg' Lowen, running things at Greenwich with a skeleton crew. Items of major importance were quickly removed to safe storage, mainly in Somerset. The Admiralty requisitioned the still unconverted East Wing for its 'M' Branch, or 'Secret Books' department (until 1947), and both Naval Constructors and a large detachment of Wrens (WRNS) also moved into other parts of the buildings. The latter eventually used the Queen's House too, which narrowly escaped major bomb damage. This photograph is one of very few recording the wartime display in the Hall and adjacent north rooms of the House. Little else is known but it appears to have focused on the defence of merchant shipping, which had proved vital in World War I and was doing so again. The north windows onto the terrace are on the left, with the North-East Parlour beyond.

D9469-070

The Hall, 1969

The Hall here holds more exhibits but is otherwise much as when the Museum first opened in 1937. In the early years a number of 17th-century wooden chairs and similar furniture were obtained to reduce the bareness of the House, which would originally have had wall hangings and a limited amount of upholstered furniture. The niche and roadway door were re-formed in 1935 based on a sketch plan of about 1661, and John James's later one: previously a larger door led into a corridor at Hall floor level under the Centre Bridge. Daniel Mytens's portrait of Charles Howard, 1st Earl of Nottingham, Lord Admiral against the Armada in 1588, was presented to Greenwich Hospital by George IV and is in its 1937 position. To far left, over the iron 'Chatham Chest' (which held the funds of the earliest seamen's charity, established about 1590) is Willem van de Velde the Younger's painting of the *Gouden Leeuw* at the Battle of the Texel in 1673, purchased in 1952 from the Earl of Halifax. The paintings on the gallery by Matteo Perez d'Aleccio once belonged to Charles I and show the Turkish siege of Malta in 1565. The 1650s Dutch votive ship model remained hanging where shown until the late 1970s.

H0916

Part of the early attempts to bring back an impression of the top floor of the House as an inhabited space, with papered walls and period furniture. Most of the pieces shown here are probably from among those lent from the reserve collections of the Victoria and Albert Museum, and eventually returned in the early 1980s.

The stone fire surround, still in place but now painted, was one of those made during the 1930s restoration of the House. The room at this time was displaying 17th-century Dutch paintings. The large one over the fire is of an action between a Dutch squadron and Barbary corsairs, painted about 1670, by Lieve

Pietersz. Verschuier. On the right of the door leading through to the antechamber is a view of shipping off Hoorn by Bonaventura Peeters (1634) and a battle of the First Dutch War (1652–54) by Reinier Nooms.

H0918

In November 2010 HM The Queen became the last survivor of those who had attended the Museum's – and the House's – formal opening in 1937. She has made regular visits since to mark various notable occasions. These two photographs are nearly 40 years apart.

TOP: Signing the royal visitors' book in the Great Hall in 1951, at the public opening of the Museum's East Wing following its conversion as galleries after wartime use by the Admiralty. Lord Stanhope (left), the founding Chairman of Trustees, had held that position since 1928 and would retire in 1954. Reginald Lowen (right) was effectively second-in-command to both the first and second Directors (the latter being Frank Carr from 1947) until he retired in 1960.

BELOW: Inspecting the 1660s Queen's Bedchamber at the reopening of the House in its refurnished incarnation in 1990. The others shown are (left to right): Admiral of the Fleet Lord Lewin, Chairman of Trustees (1987–95), and Museum staff members Erica Davies and Alan Stimson. The latter managed the 1984–90 restoration project, with the former assisting in a research capacity.

D9455-2, D4994–032

New directions

Since 1990 the House has had a new role, for corporate and private hire. The Government only actively began to encourage commercial enterprise by national museums in the 1980s. Both the Hall and the Orangery, with their adjacent rooms, are well suited to hire uses and have proved very popular. The Hall can hold up to 120 people for a formal dinner, and more for a standing event. The South-East Parlour and Great Hall are licensed for weddings, which often use the Hall for receptions; particularly in summer, the south side of the House and the colonnades make a fine location for photography. The House is also used as a film and commercial photography location, and as a venue for various cultural events. Since 2001 its main use has been to display the National Maritime Museum art collection. Apart from marine paintings, this includes the largest portrait collection in England after that of the National Portrait Gallery. The new displays installed in 2016 also include a wide range of applied and decorative art, amounting to over 400 items in all.

F5210-017, L3431-027 (p. 111)

Into a new century

When the Queen's House was conceived in 1616, its setting was entirely a landscape of river-valley fields and marshes. Today, as the House enters its fifth century, Greenwich Park and Blackheath to the south are a small green island in a vast sea of buildings, beyond the imagination of the age of Inigo Jones. Seen from the Park, however, the House still forms the frontispiece to a larger complex behind – although for the last 250 years this has been Wren's former naval Hospital, rather than the sprawling red-brick palace of Henry VII and Henry VIII. However, the outline of the Park itself has changed little since the House was built and this aerial view clearly shows many of the surviving elements of Le Nôtre's 1660s redesign for Charles II. These include the tree-lined parterre to the south of the House. Further south, on the hill, the Royal Observatory today looks out over what, since 1997, has been the Maritime Greenwich World Heritage Site, of which the Queen's House is and will remain – in time, space and style – both the focus and the architectural point of origin.

F7703-064

Shown above is an evening view of the same room shown on pp. 50–51, following the year-long House refurbishment of July 2015 to October 2016, and previous conservation of the original painted ceiling in a project supported by the Foyle Foundation. The end window and others blocked off elsewhere are now open, and all 67 sash windows (comprising 695 panes) have been reglazed. This is also one of many rooms in which the damaged and worn 1930s oak floorboards have been replaced with new French oak, laid in the traditional manner of wide runs at the centre, narrowing towards the sides. Modern furniture, with historically inspired fabrics, has also been added throughout the House for visitor use, and a new but historically based decorative scheme undertaken. The three paintings on the left are temporary loans: that over the fire of Charles I and Henrietta Maria by Daniel Mytens is one of several from the Royal Collection. On the right is the 'Armada Portrait' of Elizabeth I, acquired in 2016.

S0209-11

The various historical quotations used in the text have not been specifically referenced, but those relating to the House occur in one or more of the following:

John Bold, *Greenwich: an Architectural History of the Royal Hospital for Seamen and the Queen's House* (London and New Haven, 2000)

George H. Chettle, *The Queen's House, Greenwich* (London, 1937)

Vaughan Hart, *Inigo Jones: the Architect of Kings* (London and New Haven, 2011)

Gordon Higgott, 'The Design and Setting of Inigo Jones's Queen's House', pp. 135–48 in the *Greenwich Palace* issue of *The Court Historian*, vol. 11, no. 2, December 2006; also 'Inigo Jones's Designs for the Queen's House in 1616' in M. Airs and G. Tyacke, eds., *The Renaissance Villa in Britain, 1500–1700* (Reading, 2007).

The Queen's House: A Royal Palace by the Thames (NMM, 1990). The visitor guidebook published following the 1980s restoration of the House, this includes the best pictorial coverage of that project and the results.

There have been three good general biographies of Jones in the last century, of which the most recent is Michael Leapman, *Inigo: the Troubled Life of Inigo Jones, Architect* (London, 2003). Its predecessors, both titled *Inigo Jones*, are those of Sir John Summerson (1966) and J. A. Gotch (1928). For those with access to the *Oxford Dictionary of National Biography* (2004; and as updated online), John Newman's entry on Jones provides a concentrated synopsis and an extensive list of further sources.